Hon.

Alpheus Felch

with

Dr. Mathews' respects

THE BIBLE

AND

CIVIL GOVERNMENT,

IN A

COURSE OF LECTURES,

BY

J. M. MATHEWS, D. D.

"He that ruleth over men must be just, ruling in the fear of God."
2 Samuel, 23 : 3.

NEW-YORK:
ROBERT CARTER & BROTHERS,
285 BROADWAY.

1851.

Printed and Stereotyped
BY D. FANSHAW,
35 Ann, corner of Nassau-st.

CONTENTS.

PREFACE.

It was my original intention not to publish the following Lectures until they should appear as a part of the entire work on the connection between Science and Religion, which I am engaged in preparing. But I have been induced to change my purpose. They were delivered at the city of Washington in the early part of 1848, when the news reached this country apprising us of the commotions in Europe which have since formed a topic of absorbing interest to all intelligent observers of the times. The views which I have endeavored to illustrate on the relations of Civil Government to the Holy Scriptures, are thought to have an important bearing on the political revolutions then and still in progress; and, out of deference to the request of many for whose judgment and wishes I feel a high respect, I have decided to publish them in a volume by themselves. The circumstance of their having been delivered in the Capitol, before an audience composed chiefly of those who occupied the high places of authority in the land, may serve to show why I have made so frequent a reference to the privileges and responsibilities of our own country.

The publication of these Lectures in a separate volume, has afforded the more space for the notes which I have appended to them, and which will be acceptable to readers who may not have at hand all the authorities from which they are selected. There is one class of works to which I have referred, not only with a frequency but with a confidence, which some readers may be inclined to disapprove. I refer to the leading Periodicals of the Press, as the American and Foreign Quarterlies. On many subjects, especially such as are of high interest to the public welfare at the present time, there is no better authority extant. A new era in authorship has arisen. The generations of folios have in a great measure passed away. These "sons of Anak" no longer weigh down the shelves of libraries, or burden the arms of readers, as in former times. In their stead has arisen a generation of duodecimos and octavos, sometimes springing from the bowels of their unwieldy ancestors, and again coming into life and forming an entirely new race. Among these, our periodicals take a high stand. They are the channels through which the intellect of our day pours forth many of its best treasures. They are no longer mere finger posts, pointing us to the stores of knowledge. They contain the mine in themselves. The world is no loser by this change. There are many able men who are masters of some important questions whose knowledge would die with them, if they had not an article in some modern quarterly, or monthly, or weekly, as a means of communication with the public. The periodicals have thus become enriched with contributions to the stock of knowledge, till there is no subject in divinity or philosophy, ethics or politics, which they have not treated with great ability, and on which they do not form a valuable reference. The writers give us not only their own views, but the views of other men; and generally not diluted, but rather distilled and condensed.

Among the other authorities to which I have referred, either in the body of the Lectures or in the Notes, and to which I feel myself indebted, are, Selden De Synedriis et Præfecturis Juridicis Veterum Ebrœorum—Lowman on the Hebrew Government—Adams' Defence of the American Constitution—Paley's Moral Philosophy—Dwight's Theology—Michaelis' Commentaries on the Laws of Moses—Jahn's Archæology—Story on the Constitution of the United States—Kent's Commentaries—Chateaubriand's Beauties of Christianity—De Tocqueville's Democracy in America—Brougham's Political Philosophy—Hallam's Introduction to the Literature of the Middle Ages—Alison's History of Europe—and Macauley's History of England. To these I will add the name of Professor Wines. Although his lectures on the Hebrew Commonwealth have not yet been given from the press, they have been delivered in many of our principal cities, and have been received with an attention which was creditable to the public taste. I hope in due time to have the pleasure of reading what I have heard with profit and pleasure. The lectures of Professor Wines would form a valuable acquisition to the library of every man who wishes to become well acquainted with the Hebrew polity and the leading principles of Hebrew legislation.

I have not always coincided with the views embraced by some of the writers to whom I have referred; and I have been the more careful to express my dissent from Michaelis, in order that my reference to his authority on some questions might not be interpreted as an indication that I embrace his sentiments on others. He was a man not only of great learning, but of great pride in his learning. This led him to take positions which cannot be maintained, and also to treat the Bible itself as if he felt himself authorized rather to show what it ought to teach, than to explain what it does teach. His works contain various and valuable information, but he is an unsafe commentator for those who will not take pains to separate the chaff from the wheat.

I feel that I ought not to forego this opportunity of acknowledging the kindness of friends by which I have been enabled to pursue the work to which for some time past I have devoted myself. Subject after subject has been presented for consideration till I have been induced to enter upon fields of inquiry far beyond the limits originally contemplated; and of course the more time is required to prepare the whole work for the press. I am constantly reminded by those best qualified to judge, that investigations professing to illustrate the connection between science and religion ought to be conducted with great care and deliberation. Nothing can be gained, and much may be lost, by injudicious haste. It is not to be denied that in the contest which Christianity has been called to wage against "philosophy falsely so called," truth has too often suffered by arguments in its defence that were found in the end to be superficial and inconclusive.

Some of our distinguished scholars and divines revised and rewrote many of their most useful sermons twelve or fourteen times before publication; and if they were willing to bestow such care and diligence on discourses which treated the more familiar subjects of Christianity, I ought not to be sparing of labor and patience when pursuing investigations on the harmony between those two great departments of knowledge, the Word and the Works of God.

Sincerely do I wish that the work I have before me was in abler hands than mine. I derive satisfaction from the hope that I shall be followed by those who will supply my deficiencies. "Every age," says a distinguished writer, "as well as every individual, has its specific duty; and the duty of the nineteenth century is to bring science, in all its discoveries, to bear upon religion, and to corroborate, if we may so speak, the Word of God." There seems to be a wide spread conviction of this important truth among intelligent Christians. But although the attention of able scientific men has been turned to the subject, the adequate illustration of the Scriptures by the discoveries of science is a work only just begun. Much, much remains to be done before learning shall have paid the debt which she owes to the volume of inspiration. The christian scholar should never rest satisfied till every discovery in the world of nature is laid at the foot of His altars, who is "the Way, the Truth, and the Life." Although I may be able to do but little in carrying forward so important a service, I should feel grateful if allowed to have any part in it; nor do I know how I could be more usefully employed, than in fulfilling the task which in this view I have prescribed to myself.

INTRODUCTORY LECTURE.

The capacity of nations for self-government is one of the great questions of the age. Fresh discussions of it are prompted by events which follow each other in such rapid succession as to resemble the ever-varying figures and colors of the kaleidescope. Governments in the old world, which had endured for centuries, have fallen into a state of dilapidation; and, in some instances, their foundations have been destroyed by convulsions, which required but a single day for their entire overthrow. To an extent seldom witnessed before, we have seen the Scripture fulfilled—"Remove the diadem, and take off the crown: this shall not be the same: exalt him that is low, and abase him that is high. I will overturn, overturn, overturn it; and it shall be no more, until He come whose right it is; and I will give it

Him." In the midst of this removal of diadems and these wide-spreading revolutions, men very properly inquire as to what must be the result when the people are thus aiming to take civil power into their own hands, and claim to be governed under forms and rulers of their own choice. As may be inferred from the words of the prophet just quoted, the question is intimately connected, not only with the stability of just government, but with the spread of the Gospel; and every one who is the friend of his race and of Christianity, should be willing to contribute his aid to illustrate its importance and defend it from error and abuse. In all great changes which affect social or political organizations of long standing, there is danger of rashness and excess; and in breaking away from one set of evils, communities sometimes rush into others of an opposite character, but still more disastrous tendency.

Men always become vain in their imaginations when they turn away from the word of God, and neglect to hear it in relation to any subject on which it condescends to give us instruction. A distinguished author has of late entitled one of his best Essays "The Bible the best guide to political skill and foresight;" and it is to be viewed among the redeeming signs of the times, that public men and profound thinkers are turning increased attention to the inspired volume, not only as a revelation of mercy to fallen man, but as a record of the cardinal principles of wisdom and equity which should enter into the government of nations. Happy will it be for all lands when their rulers will take increasing counsel from "the Father of Lights" "by whom princes decree justice," both as to the source of their authority over men, and the manner in which it should be exercised. This would be another step towards the promised consummation, when "nation shall not lift up sword against nation, neither shall they learn war any more." Not a few of those who are counted among our leading statesmen have become deeply impressed with these convictions; and at their suggestion, I have endeavored in the following Lectures to illustrate

The connection between the Holy Scriptures and the Science of Civil Government.

I am far from supposing that I can do full justice to the subject. I approach it as an expositor of Scriptural truth, not as a statesman or a jurist; and I shall feel rewarded if I may be the means of leading the minds of abler and more accomplished men to develope it at greater length and to more perfection.

The tradition that Divine authority was requisite

to establish laws, or a government of laws over a people, was very general during the ages of antiquity. The belief also seems to have been most widely diffused wherever civilization and refinement had made the greatest advancement. The laws of Crete were said to have been given to Minos by inspiration from Jupiter. Apollo, we are told, revealed the laws of Lacedæmon to Lycurgus; and to ensure a just interpretation of them, the deity allowed himself to be consulted from time to time at the Oracle of Delphos. Numa declared himself indebted to Egeria for the statutes and ordinances which lay at the foundation of Roman greatness and supremacy. Referring to the general prevalence of such traditions, an able commentator on government has remarked, "there is nothing in which mankind have been more unanimous." But while we fully agree with him as to the fact, we entirely dissent from him when he adds, "yet nothing can be inferred from it, but that the multitude have always been credulous, and the few artful." The unanimity of the belief, leads, as we think, to quite a different conclusion. Sound philosophy has discovered, that in all such traditions there is a mixture of truth with error; that there is scarce a fable to be found in the mythologies of ancient times without a "moral," which can be traced back to some revelation previously derived from the true God. Accordingly we consider these fictions or fables respecting the origin of civil laws as another acknowledgment of the truth so conspicuously repeated in the Scriptures, that "there is no power but of God;" that "the powers that be are ordained of God;" in other words, that the obligation of the ruled to obey their rulers rests upon the Divine will as its great and ultimate reason.

But while there is a general concurrence among moral and political writers in the doctrine that civil government is founded on the will of God, they are by no means so fully agreed respecting the extent to which he has revealed his will on the subject. And the object which we now propose to ourselves is to inquire how far the Scriptures go, in revealing the essential principles which enter into a just and wise construction of the civil authority which man may rightfully exercise over man. We turn "to the law and to the testimony," and ask, Is government, simply as government, all that we find there sanctioned as the ordinance of God; and have its different forms been left to be elaborated by the sagacity of politicians and statesmen, all of them sharing alike in the Divine approbation? Do the Autocrat of Russia, and the Sultan of Turkey, inheriting thrones which have been gained by violence and blood, hold their power by a tenure as scriptural as the chief Magistrates of these United States, who have been raised to their office by the choice of those whom they govern?

The Bible, if we do not mistake its meaning, answers these inquiries in a way that may well render it increasingly valuable in the eyes of every one who desires the present and future happiness of his race. As we follow its teachings, we find it goes back into the antiquity of nations, and records their origin and progress, with a clearness to which no other volume can aspire. It shows that the form of government first prevailing in the world was the patriarchal. And while the earth was peopled rather by families than by nations, dominion in the hands of one man might not have been productive of any oppressive wrongs. But when communities had become widened into large kingdoms, ties of kindred were lost in ambition for power; and tyranny, with its unsparing exactions, was soon felt as the scourge of humanity. Then, as the Scriptures teach, the Most High made known a remedy for this sore evil. But it is not his manner to ordain mere abstractions when he gives ordinances for the benefit of man. If government of any kind is to be rendered intelligible or tangible, it must have some form or embodiment; and as "at the beginning," he taught how the domestic relations were to be created and sustained; so also, when nations "had begun to multiply on the earth," he revealed his will respecting the origin and tenure of authority in a State, showing how the relations between rulers and ruled should be formed and regulated. When he "brought the Hebrews out of the land of Egypt, out of the house of bondage," his first care was to give them laws and ordinances by which he made known his redeeming grace for lost man. But he did not forget their temporal welfare as a Nation, while he guided their faith as his Church. *He formed them into a Commonwealth under civil enactments, which embrace all the essential features of national freedom, or of a well-ordered Republic.*

This religious aspect of the subject enhances its claim upon our careful consideration. And is it not fitting and seasonable that civil liberty should be more fully rescued from the profanity with which it has been too often treated? Notwithstanding what we view as an improved state of opinion in some quarters, there is still much public impiety with regard to this inestimable blessing; impiety which pollutes our seats of learning, and profanes our high places of authority. Our educated youth are still taught to believe, and the people are still told by many of our public men, that liberty was cradled in the states of Greece; and that the Solons and Lycurguses of former days were the great fathers of freedom to our world. We believe in a different doctrine. We believe that we must look further back than either Athens or Sparta for the origin of a blessing most deeply interwoven with the welfare of man; and that it was not the wisdom of Greece in the halls of the Acropolis, but the wisdom of God speaking from heaven through his servant Moses, which first taught how the rights of a people should be asserted and sustained.

While impiety is rebuked, unbelief may at the same time be put to shame. There are Cassandras, croaking prophets in our own country, who are always predicting the speedy overthrow of our free institutions; and there are Catalines and Hotspurs who would love to have it so, as it would open to them the fields of treachery and blood in which they delight. But there are men also of sober and reflecting minds, who look on the future both abroad and at home with much anxiety. "Upon the earth there is distress of nations, with perplexity, men's hearts failing them for fear, and for looking after those things that are coming upon the earth." Far and near we see a tumult of kingdoms, in which "deep calleth unto deep;" and the responses are loud and portentous. Great as the changes may be which we have seen taking place, they are pregnant with others still greater which must soon follow. They are only "the beginning of the end," and there may be many fluctuations between good and evil before that end can be reached. The fates of empires seem to be governed by new laws which baffle the wisdom of the wise, and turn "the counsels of Ahithophels into foolishness." Every institution that has sprung from the ambition or the policy of man, seems tending toward a general wreck; and the efforts of statesmen to prevent the catastrophe, seem only to accelerate it. The gigantic strength of the popular will is, Samson-like, heaving at the pillars of a tyranny that has long doomed men to blindness as well as to bondage; but it too often threatens, in its maddened violence, to bring ruin both on the oppressed and the oppressors; while the "Lords of the Philistines" infatuated with the love of power, and bewildered by the dread of losing it, are running into measures that must render their overthrow the more fearful when the day of retribution comes. Nor are the commotions and changes of our day confined to the political world. The fountains of every great deep, whether in church or state, are fast being broken up, as if to issue in another deluge that shall overthrow every thing that has been heretofore viewed as high and stable. The corrupting alliances with worldly pomp and power, which have long burdened Christianity, are beginning to give way; but we fear they must be wrenched by many a rude, if not bloody hand, before they can be finally severed. Gross superstitions, which have degraded Christianity down to the verge of Paganism, and the blind idolatries of Paganism itself, are sinking into decrepitude and discredit. Mahomedanism can no longer claim the Crescent as its emblem. Its moon is also on the wane. But, although the forms of irreligion and error are losing their sway, we must not believe that they can be finally overthrown without further struggle; and in the mean time the spirit of change which at first may have been an ambition for healthful reform, too often degenerates into a blasphemous impiety; and instead of a meretricious faith, embraces a licentious infidelity, that mocks at truth and at the God of truth.

Nor should we in this brief review pass by in silence disquieting indications which we find at home. We have here "the largest liberty for the largest number;" but it is too often perverted and abused by men who display a lawless and rabid hostility against many of our best institutions, both civil and religious. "Deceiving and being deceived, despising dominion, and speaking evil of dignities," they carry with them a hardened and unblushing ambition to pull down every thing which is built up, to unsettle every thing that has been settled either by the authority of God or the matured wisdom of man; and under the guise of a benevolence that promises to render all men free and equal, they would subvert every obligation of justice which binds society together, and every sense of truth and duty that should bind us all in reverence to our Creator.

It should not be denied that these "signs of the times," which are so widely spread, are the ominous mutterings of a coming tempest. They are notes of preparation for a war which, as we are told in the Sriptures, is to convulse our world previous to the millenial reign of Him who is Prince of Peace and Saviour of our fallen race. In the language of prophecy, "the angel" seems to be "pouring out his vial into the air," and it is followed by "voices, and thunders, and lightnings." Opposing hosts are fast becoming marshalled for what may well be called "the battle of the great day," great in reference both to the magnitude of the interests involved and the forces engaged; and when infidelity may perhaps be found in strange alliance with superstition and tyranny against Christianity and freedom. It will not be a strife for some portion of territory or some conventional point of national honor; but for the unalienable rights that belong to man created in the image of his Maker. It will be a war between the oppressors and the oppressed, between the doers of wrong and the sufferers of wrong, between the long established usages which bind men to the chariot wheels of civil and ecclesiastical domination, and their fresh born and holy purpose, to see for themselves and act for themselves in the momentous concerns "of the life which now is, and of that which is to come."

With such a crisis impending, it is both natural and dutiful that we should set ourselves to survey with care the tenure by which we, as a people, hold the privileges which we enjoy, and which are so soon to be put at stake. How far we may be hereafter drawn into the coming struggle time must show. But the subject at present comes home to us in an aspect by no means equivocal. The duty and the destiny of America seem to have been written in a book that is yet but partially unsealed. Enough is known, however, to indicate that she is to act no subordinate part in the great events now "casting their shadows before them." It is obvious that there are two great powers which now stand prominently before the world as the distinct impersonations of despotism on the one hand, and of liberty on the other. They are the Russian Empire in the Old World, and the United States of America in the New. They are both constantly widening their borders, and augmenting their resources, as if gathering fresh accessions of strength for some gigantic conflict. Recent events too are bringing them more fully upon the confines of each other; and in these times remarkable for setting at defiance the ordinary calculations of politicians, some collision of interests on our own continent may yet place the two Powers in open hostility.* But although such an event may be counted among bare possibi-

* It is now fifteen years since the following observations were made by M. De Tocqueville in his work entitled "Democracy in America." Events which have since transpired tend to show how well he understood the position and character of the two countries.

"There are," he remarks, "at the present time, two great nations in the world, which seem to tend towards the same end, although they started from different points I allude to the Russians and Americans. Both of them have grown up unnoticed: and whilst the attention of mankind was directed elsewhere, they have suddenly assumed a most prominent place amongst the nations; and the world learned their greatness and existence at almost the same time.

"All other nations seem to have nearly reached their natural limits, and only to be charged with the maintenance of their power; but these are still in the act of their growth: all the others are stopped, or continue to advance with extreme difficulty; these are proceeding with ease and with celerity along a path to which the human eye can assign no term.—The Anglo-American relies upon

lities, our country is considered by general consent as the home and the citadel of civil freedom in a sense peculiar to itself; and as such is viewed with a jealous eye by many of the crowned heads of Europe. They have long consoled themselves with the belief that we would prove our own worst enemies, that our experiment of self-government would end in anarchy and blood; and every trifling outbreak between neighbors has been hailed as an omen that these sinister predictions were about to be fulfilled. There is one sure ground of hope. "If God be for us, who can be against us?" If we hold our free institutions from God; and if, after the example of our fathers,* we embalm them in our prayers as a gift from him, and are faithful to the trust he has reposed in us, then shall we still continue to possess them. They shall be ours from generation to generation. But if they come only from man, we have no such security. They may pass from us as a dream, and come to naught. May I not therefore hope to carry with me

personal interest to accomplish his ends, and gives free scope to the unguided exertions and common sense of the citizens; the Russians centre all the authority of society in a single arm: the principle instrument of the former is freedom; of the latter servitude. Their starting-point is different, and their courses are not the same; yet each of them seems to be marked out by the will of Heaven to sway the destinies of half the globe."

* Note A.

the attention of rulers and ruled who hear me, while I endeavor to show the Divine origin of civil freedom?

Before entering upon the argument taken immediately from the Scriptures themselves, I would ask you to consider,

How fitly it corresponds with the uniform goodness of God, that he should give to the world a distinct revelation of his will on this subject. "Thy commandment is exceeding broad," says the Psalmist. There is an expansive power in the Bible which reaches every want and condition in life. Sometimes as in the Decalogue, and in the "Golden Rule," of "doing to others as we would that others should do unto us," it states great general principles of duty in such brief language that young and old may remember them and carry them about as household words. But it does not stop here. It goes on to teach how these comprehensive precepts should be applied to the various relations, whether domestic, social or civil, which the well-being of society requires that men should sustain to each other. And we may here add, that unless the relations of rulers and of ruled are wisely regulated, men can have no security in either their social or domestic enjoyments. As tyranny existed in the world when the Hebrews were brought out of Egypt, it had become the sorest earthly curse that could afflict our race, and one from which they could devise no adequate means of escape. If you would see how the despotism of that day carried bitterness and death into families and nations, let us take a survey of the cruelties then occurring every hour under the sceptre of the Pharaohs. Among the people of the Hebrews every "life was made bitter by hard bondage." But though driven to "make bricks without straw," this was but a small part of the suffering inflicted on them by their unfeeling king. How wide and heart-rending was the cry of anguish heard from every dwelling where "a son is born." It was like the "voice in Ramah," "Rachel weeping for her children, and would not be comforted because they were not." The royal mandate had been issued, ordaining "every son that is born of a Hebrew woman, ye shall cast into the river;" and so rigidly was the command enforced that the Nile became a vast sepulchre for new-born babes; and the house of the bereaved mother was converted into a home of sorrow and tears by the cruel death of those whose lives would have rendered it the abode of gladness and mirth. And this, be it remembered, is but an example of the oppression and wrong which then afflicted all nations of the earth. Every where, the lives, the happiness, and the liberty of the subject, were at the will of the one man who wore the crown; and who, drunk with the possession of irresponsible power, ruled over men as over the beasts of the field. Surely there was much in a degradation and wretchedness like this, rendering it fit for Him whose " tender mercies are over all his works," to show how a nation may be governed so as best to guard against such grievous and consuming ills.

But farther: let us look at the influence of freedom on those higher faculties of man which reach beyond his domestic enjoyments. The sentiment so beautifully expressed,

> " 'Tis liberty alone that gives the flower
> " Of fleeting life its lustre and perfume,"

is verified by the history of nations, whether ancient or modern. History never misleads. It " is Philosophy teaching by example." Let us turn to it, and learn in what countries and under what kind of government the intellectual and moral faculties which adorn and dignify our nature have been most happily developed.

Allow me here to quote from a work among the most able in our language, and well known as a most unbending advocate of royalty and rank for perfecting the body politic. " Civilized democracy," it tells us, " is the great moving power in human affairs; the source of the greatest efforts of human genius; and when duly restrained from running into excess, the grand instrument of human advancement. Its grand characteristic is energy, and energy not rousing the exertions merely of a portion of society, but awakening the dormant strength of millions; not producing merely the chivalrous valor of the high bred cavalier, but drawing forth the might that slumbers in a peasant's arm. The greatest achievements of genius, the noblest efforts of heroism that have illustrated the history of the species have arisen from the influence of this principle. Thence the fight of Marathon and the glories of Salamis—the genius of Greece and the conquests of Rome—the heroism of Sempach and the devotion of Harlæm—the paintings of Raphael and the poetry of Tasso—the energy that covered with a velvet carpet the slopes of the Alps, and the industry which bridled the stormy seas of the German ocean. Why are the shores of the Mediterranean the scene to which the pilgrim from every quarter of the globe journeys to visit, at once, the cradles of civilization, the birthplace of arts, of arms, of philosophy, of poetry, and the scenes of their highest and most glorious achievements? Because freedom spread along its smiling shores; because the ruins of Athens and Sparta, of Rome and Carthage, of Tyre and Syracuse lie on its margin; because civilization advancing with the white sails which glittered on its blue expanse, pierced, as if impelled by central heat, through the dark and barbarous regions of the Celtic race who peopled its shores.—What gave Rome the empire of the world, and brought the venerable ensigns, bearing the words, "Senatus populusque Romanus," (the senate and the people of Rome,) to the wall of Antoninus, and the foot of the Atlas, the waters of the Euphrates and the Atlantic ocean?—Republican Rome colonized the world; republican Greece spread the light of civilization along the shores of the Mediterranean. But Imperial Rome could never maintain the number of its own provinces; and the Grecian Empire slumbered on with a declining population for eleven hundred years."*

Eloquent and glowing as these extracts may be regarded, they are not exaggerated or fanciful. They present a faithful picture of truth. There are but few green spots in our fallen world where man has ever made any great advancement in whatever most elevates his nature and improves his happiness. Among these, as we shall hereafter show, the land of the Hebrews stands first among ancient nations. But whether it be Palestine, Greece or Rome,

* Blackwood, January, 1836. The article from which the extracts are taken is entitled "The Future," and will amply repay a careful perusal.

of former ages; whether it be Genoa, Venice, Holland or England, of later times, the germ, at least, of civil freedom, was found in them all; and though its growth may at times have been retarded, and its beauty marred by unnatural restraints and entanglements, yet just in proportion as these antagonist forces were removed or overcome, did the struggling spirit of freedom impart a healthful activity to the noblest powers and aspirations of man. What an impulse, for instance, was given to knowledge and refinement in the free States of Italy, when they were liberated from tyranny? There, it may be said, learning and art first raised their heads, after their fearful overthrow by the invasion of the northern barbarians. What was Holland before she became freed from both ecclesiastical and civil domination? With few exceptions, the minds of her people were as stagnant as the waters in her boundless marshes. There was no nerve in the national arm to bridle the waves of the ocean from overflowing her shores; there were no fleets issuing from her ports to come back enriching her with the wealth of the world; no seminaries of learning teeming with a growth of intellect that rendered the divines, the physicians, the lawyers, the statesmen, the philosophers of Holland, the oracles of their day throughout the civilized world. But soon as she acquired her national independence and freedom, she raised herself to a first rank among nations in all these high attainments; and has enabled her descendants among us to look back upon her with high reverence for their "fatherland."

Or shall we look at another country to which, as a people, we can trace a more general ancestry? Mark the stages of progress made by England, as a birthplace of knowledge, refinement and high enterprise for public good; and you will see that just according as arbitrary power, whether in king or nobles, has been checked and over-ruled by the spirit of civil freedom in her people, her course has been onward. What was she before her Magna Charta was granted and signed as her first great step of disenthralment from bondage? Her curfew bell was rung every night, as if to proclaim the darkness that covered the land, and to remind her of the iron sceptre that controlled her every hour and her best enjoyments. But what has she become since that day of her first release; and especially since the seeds of liberty took their deep root in her soil during the commonwealth, and have become developed and embodied in her far-famed Bill of Rights? There she sits like a star in the lap of the ocean. Her name and her power are known wherever the sun shines; and her achievements have placed her first among the nations of Europe in all that the wise most seek to know, or the good most desire to do.

But let us turn at once to our own country. Here, as all admit, freedom has a dwelling which is "like a city set upon a hill, which cannot be hid." Compare her as she is here, with what she was in Greece or Rome. There she was defaced by deformities inseparable from the darkness of Paganism. Here she has acquired the symmetry and beauty which could be derived only from the moulding power of Christianity. No such thing as genuine freedom can be enjoyed by a people who are divided from each other by those iron bands of caste which are interwoven with the structure of society in Pagan lands. Christianity alone has power to melt down such instruments of cruelty and injustice. It teaches the doctrine that "God hath made of one blood all nations that dwell on the face of the earth," and lays its command on every man to "love his neighhor as himself." From these two cardinal principles it enforces that safe equality which preserves the social fabric from dissolution, and at the same time renders the rights of the weakest and strongest equally secure. If it levels distinctions among men, it levels upward, not downward; it elevates the low, elevates them in mind and in conduct; and so far as it brings down the high, it brings down nothing but those "vain imaginations which exalt themselves against God." This is the equality which our free institutions, imbued with the spirit of the Bible, are designed to effect. The Roman patrician knew nothing of it, nor did he act upon it. Had you told him that he was sprung from the same dust as the humble plebeian, he would have laughed you to scorn.

We might also compare freedom as she is here with what we find her in Christian nations of modern times, but who weaken her influence by unnatural alliance. Here she is not overshadowed and dwarfed in her growth by her proximity to towering royalty. She has the field to herself. She places sovereignty in the hands of the people, and sends them to the Bible, that they may learn how to wear the crown.

And what has been the effect of her christianized and untrammeled sway during little more than half a century, on the condition of the nation? Where do you find intelligence, enterprise, industry, competency, and a respect for religion, if not acquaintance with its power, so general as you find them here? Where such a growth in whatsoever is most essential to public greatness? Every thing rests on the diffusion of sound intelligence through the mass of the people, on the cultivation of a just standard of right and wrong among all classes; and every where we have the school and the church, the teacher and the preacher, as the great fountains of light and truth to the nation. The result of such training is not to be questioned or overlooked. The observing stranger has passed through our country, and describes it as "a land of wonders, in which every thing is in constant motion, and every movement seems an improvement; a land where no natural boundary seems to be set to the efforts of man; and what is not yet done, is only what he has not yet attempted to do." It is the mind of a whole nation teeming with purposes for advancement in knowledge and in the power which knowledge gives. As a people, activity is our element. Idlers find themselves alone. They can meet with neither company nor countenance. The mind of every man is acting on the mind of his neighbor, thus stimulating the faculties of both to accomplish new objects and make new discoveries in the still unexplored regions of nature and of art. In illustration of this quickened and irrepressible activity, let us refer to one or two of those inventions which, acting in correspondence with the spirit of our age, are destined to work an entire change in the condition of nations, whether "Barbarian or Scythian, bond or free."

It has been well observed that when great improvements are about to be made in human affairs, some powerful agency is provided adequate to the end, and adapted to the occasion. Prior to the reformation came the art of printing; that being an era in the history of the world, in which a new impulse was to be given to the spread of knowledge among civilized nations. We are now on the verge of another era, in which "the field is to be the world;" in which Christianity is to be carried over every sea and through every land of the globe; in which, to use the language of prophesy,* "many shall run to and fro, and knowledge shall be increased." For the accomplishment of this great end, we need some new instrumentality for speeding communication between the various regions of the earth; and which, for all moral purposes, shall bring the most distant nations into close neighborhood one with another. We see this wonder-working power in the recent applications of steam and electricity, which are fast annihilating both time and space. By means of the one, our vessels move on the waters in the face of the winds, and with a speed that outstrips them; and our cars pass over the land with a swiftness that leaves our vessels far behind them. By means of the other, intelligence is sent to the terminus of the railroad, though distant thousands of miles, giving notice that the cars have just begun to move. It is through these newly discovered agencies, that seas and lands, although hitherto unexplored, are soon to become the pathways of truth and knowledge; and the good news of "Glory to God in the highest, on earth peace and good will towards men," are to be borne "to the utmost borders of the earth." A new longevity is bestowed on man, for the length of his life is to be measured by his power of doing good; and he can now accomplish in a day what formerly would have cost the tedious labor of months. The lever is prepared for human hands which is to do more than the lever of Archimedes. It is not only to move the world, but to transform and cover it with the light of truth. And where were these inventions first made available for the great purposes they are now answering? Whatever may be said respecting the claims of Holland to the credit of having invented the art of printing while cherishing the seeds of a republic; it cannot be denied, that in our own land of freedom, the Steamer and the Telegraph have been nurtured into activity and usefulness; and the work has been done mainly, not by men of any privileged class, but by those who sprung from the multitude; and whose faculties, sharpened by a sense of self-reliance, persevered against ridicule, wrong, and even want, till their object was gained.

The same spirit of achievement is seen in other

branches of knowledge, which has so happily displayed itself in the useful arts. The time has gone by when even the mocker would dare to ask, Who reads an American book? How rapidly our Bench and our Bar have risen to eminence during the last half century; and how liberal have been their contributions to the great store-house of legal knowledge, is acknowledged wherever jurisprudence is understood and appreciated. If I may speak of my own profession, our divines, according to their numbers, have done their part to vindicate and illustrate the great truths of the Gospel. But our distinguishing achievement in religion is that in which as a people we yet stand alone. Nor is it to be traced simply to the wisdom of our divines, or of any one profession or class of our citizens. It is the result of public sentiment pervading the land. We have severed the Church from the State. We have withdrawn and secured religion, the holiest boon of heaven, from corrupting alliance with civil authority. We have discovered, if discovery it can be called, that religion is best supported when self-supported. We have brought to the proof of successful experiment, what was long ridiculed as a dream, that those who enjoy the blessings of Christianity, will best sustain her worship and ordinances by their voluntary offerings. We ask neither establishment nor toleration from the

State. We require nothing but protection for all worshippers, and in any form of worship which conscience approves, and which will not disturb the peace and safety of others. I dwell on this subject the more because it so well exemplifies the fearless and truth-loving spirit of inquiry which belongs to our nation. The belief that religion could be sustained only by the patronage of the State, was indurated by the rust of ages. It formed an article in Protestant as well as Papal creeds. The Reformation, with all its power in dispelling delusions and removing abuses, had failed to create a reformed and scriptural faith on this important point, important both to the peace of the State, and the purity and prosperity of the Church. In this country we broke down ecclesiastical establishments when we broke away from colonial dependence. We made the Church independent of the State when we wrought out the independence of the nation. We have based the claims of religion for support on her own excellence, as she herself reveals it to the hearts of men; and now, having watched the working of our system for more than half a century, we find the result to be most propitious. We find it in the liberality with which the ministry and ordinances of the Gospel are sustained. In no land throughout Protestant Christendom are the clergy, as a class, placed in circumstances of a more happy competency than in these United States. If none of them are luxuriating in princely incomes, none of them are left destitute of the necessaries of life. We find it also in the spirit of mutual kindness and good will which prevails among the various denominations of Christians. "Judah does not vex Ephraim, nor does Ephraim envy Judah." No one sect, because established by law, can look down upon others who do not enjoy the same patronage. We all share equally in the favor of the State, and must all depend equally on ourselves for favor among the people. We find it also in the enlarged munificence and increased activity with which our churches act, for the spread of the Gospel. Universal experience shows, that it is those whose hearts are trained to liberality by sustaining religion among themselves, who lead the way in voluntary offerings for sending it to others.

Not to cite farther proofs showing the vigor with which the minds of our people act, in new acquisitions of knowledge, and in correcting old and long established errors and abuses; let me now ask, what can it be that gives to the nation this elastic spirit, this indomitable energy and perseverance! What, that diffuses this character so widely as to make it extend to every class, in every condition of life? No doubt we owe it to our wide spread Christianity as the first and great cause. But had Christianity been cramped and enfeebled by civil disabilities and restraints, she would have been far from imparting this tone to the public mind. She has long existed under these counteracting influences in lands where we find but little proof of such power on the character of the people. No, it is only where Christianity is allowed to act herself out; to act in alliance with civil and religious freedom; a freedom which she sanctions by her own high authority; that she can "have free course," reaching all classes and imbuing a whole community with a spirit which renders them alike blessed in themselves, and the instrument of blessing to the world around them.

Surely then, if freedom is thus interwoven with the improvement and happiness of our race, it may well be expected that whatever is essential to its establishment should be revealed in a volume which "has the promise of the life that now is, and of that which is to come." The precious Book has assured us that "the hairs of our head are all numbered;" that our "bread shall be given us and our water shall be sure;" and when we are taught that the Most High governs with such care in the minutest concerns of human life, can we suppose that he would fail to instruct men in the nature and importance of institutions by which every thing valuable in their personal, domestic, civil and Christian welfare, is so deeply affected.

I would not close this Lecture without asking you to reflect, that this desire for progress, this onward spirit which I have described as characteristic of our nation, unless wisely regulated may lead into errors of no ordinary magnitude. Let it not be supposed that we would have the elastic spring of the bow destroyed, because owing to unskilful hands it may sometimes send the arrow beyond the mark. Wrong, oppression and injustice have been so long prevalent in our fallen world, that inveterate evils are not always to be eradicated, nor great benefits acquired and secured by powers of action that have been tamed down to what some would call a safe mediocrity; and if the sultry and deadly atmosphere can be purified by nothing short of the breeze freshening into a gale; then let the wind blow, and even, if need be, let the thunder roll, though the trees of the forest be shaken, and some of their branches be scattered in the storm. But while we would not have the energy of our people subdued or destroyed, we desire to see it wisely governed, and their eyes opened to the dangers which beset them.

There is danger of their being carried away by a spirit of recklessness and presumption. We have seen this too often, and especially in the crowded thoroughfares of business and of ambition, where men, excited by emulation and collision with each other, venture they know not where, until all is left to the hazard of the die. This gambling, whether for power or for wealth, is demoralizing. It blunts every sensibility to that which is right and commendable, and opens a door to temptation in its worst forms. " I, wisdom, dwell with prudence ;" and no prize, however splendid in appearance, is worth the cost, if it is gained by disregarding the dictates of either the one or the other.

We should also be on our guard against a spirit of pride and self-sufficiency, which would undervalue and repudiate much that is venerable from its age and long-tried worth. If our growth, as a people, has been rapid, we are yet young. We have yet much to gain before we can reach the grace and symmetry of nations much older than ourselves. We should be careful not to glide into the false notion that every thing which is old is also worthless. Many of the elements of our own happiness and prosperity are derived from nations now venerable for their years and time-honored institutions. While we " prove all things," we should be careful to " hold fast that which is good;" and of things which are good, we should prize those most highly, the value of which has been tested by the experience of past ages, and which come down to us commended by the judgment of the wise and the great, who are now in their graves. Especially should we always remember with a grateful regard the country from which we have derived our language, our laws, and much of what belongs to the very essence of our civil freedom. If she once may have viewed us with feelings that were both unnatural and unkind, they have given place to a good will that is becoming more generous and more just. The speedy and constant intercourse of the present day has already corrected the mistakes of former years, and has led the two countries to a more just appreciation of each other. Let the daughter remember what the mother has done to challenge veneration and love; and let the mother rejoice in the growing beauty and strength of a daughter, who in her best deeds bestows a high commendation on her early training. Let both remember that they equally belong to that race of the human family by whose labors truth and righteousness are soon to be spread through the earth. The man is a poor interpreter of "the signs of the times," who has not learnt that to England and America, under God, belongs the foremost rank in the great service of regenerating the world. The Governments of the two countries should keep this consideration constantly before them, and every opportunity should be improved to cherish the mutual kindness and respect which befit the high work they are called unitedly to fulfil. They should view it as their mission, not to kindle the torch of war, but to act as conservators of peace; and if they ever draw the sword, it should not be against each other, but to compel nations to sheathe it who have long bathed it in blood. A war between England and America would be the heaviest calamity in this eventful age, which the pride, or vanity, or ambition of wild politicians could inflict on the world.

There is also great danger lest in this rapid course of prosperity and development, we should fall into forgetfulness of God. "Beware that thou forget not the Lord thy God,—but when thou hast eaten and art full, and hast built goodly houses and dwelt therein; and when thy herds and thy flocks multiply, and thy silver and thy gold is multiplied, and all that thou hast is multiplied; then thy heart be lifted up, and thou forget the Lord thy God, and say in thine heart, My power and the might of my hand has gotten me this wealth." To no nation, not even to Israel, prosperous as they were, could this admonition be more applicable than to ourselves as a people. Our prosperity has outstripped the predictions of the most sanguine; but forgetfulness of the Giver in his gifts, is already but too manifest among us; and I dread the prevalence of it. Whenever prosperity and success, especially in objects of public interest, crown the efforts of man, his proud heart seems inclined to ask, "Is not this great Babylon, that I have built for the house of the kingdom by the might of my power, and for the honor of my majesty." True, it is a haughty monarch, glorying in his uncontrolled and unlimited sovereignty, who stands as the recorded example of such guilt and of its consequences. But in a land where every one feels that the sovereignty belongs to the people, and that he is one of the people; and that whatever national greatness may be achieved, belongs to him as a part of the nation; there is peculiar danger that this boastful spirit may become a national and easily besetting sin. And if our pride is pictured in the example of the King of Babylon, ought we not to fear lest our doom should also be found written in the tragical end of his kingdom? Pride intoxicates while it also corrupts, making those an easy prey who might otherwise be invincible. It ruled the throne of Babylon when Nebuchadnezzar no longer reigned. It taught his son to "lift up himself against the Lord of heaven;" and to abandon himself to scenes of revelry and profanity, leaving the gates of the city unguarded, until they were entered by the victorious Medes and Persians. "The fingers of a man's hand," which wrote his doom "on the plaster of the wall," have repeated the warning ever since; and from the day when that once proud and powerful empire, "the beauty of the Chaldees' excellency, "hardened her mind in pride," and said, "I shall be a Lady for ever—I, and none else besides me," the world has been filled with examples, both in princes and people, that "a haughty spirit goeth before a fall." May God save our nation from the sin, and then we shall be safe from its penalty.

SECOND LECTURE.

In the opening Lecture of this series, we advanced the proposition that not only is Civil Government the ordinance of God, but that the essential principles of civil freedom carry the seal of his authority; and that when nations "began to multiply on the earth," he made a revelation of his will, showing how the relation between rulers and ruled should be formed and regulated. This revelation was given when the Hebrews were brought out of Egypt. While God instructed them as his church in the great doctrines of redeeming grace, he did not overlook their welfare as a nation; but distinguished and elevated them above the kingdoms of that day, by forming them into a commonwealth under civil enactments, which embraced all the essential features of public freedom, or of a well-ordered Republic.

Before entering on the argument, we replied to the inquiry, whether civil liberty is such a blessing as to render it a fit subject for the express revelation which we assigned to it. We showed that it is in the fullest sense worthy of a revelation direct from God, because of its importance not only to the physical and social welfare of man, but to the development of his intellectual and moral faculties; and, because without it, Christianity itself is enfeebled and fettered. Indeed Christendom, far and near, seems to be waking up to this great truth. That honored class of men, the apostles of our day, the missionaries now laboring in heathen lands, are constantly sending to the churches at home, entreaties that we would pray for the spread of civil liberty, as indispensable to the "free course" of the Gospel.

We now come to the direct proof of our proposition. We may begin by an argument taken from

The nature of the case. It has passed into a maxim in the science of public morals, that men do not so much make institutions, as that institutions make men. This is one of the results which philosophy has drawn from universal history. Nations do not rise from degradation and barbarity of their own accord, unaided by some external agency above and beyond themselves. And what, let me ask, was the condition of the whole world when Moses arose as the inspired teacher and liberator of the Hebrews? Ignorance and bondage covered the human race as with the pall of death. The dominion of rulers was either acquired by the sword, or transmitted by inheritance from father to son; the people having no voice in the choice of him who was over them, more than if they had been the beasts of the field or the clods of the valley. He had risen to power without their will, and often against it. He was not of them, was not responsible to them, and claimed authority over them and over all that was theirs, unlimited and uncontrolled. The nations indeed moaned beneath the tyranny of the despotic oppression, but it was the moan of despair. Or if in their agony a hand was raised to resist cruelty and wrong, it was soon crushed and riveted down by some new and heavier chain. Few had the courage to struggle for liberation, and even when the effort was made, it was rather like the frantic writhings of a man goaded to madness, and beating himself against the walls of his cell, than the wise and rational labors which could obtain freedom, and secure it when obtained. The gloom of the picture was increased by the downward tendency of things from age to age; every change being only from bad to worse; and this change affecting rulers as well as ruled, making the one more corrupt, as it made the other more wretched. Indeed, such must always be the effect of despotism on the despot himself. The possession of power without responsibility might corrupt an angel. It was their grasping after it that caused angels to fall, and converted them into fiends. We can then readily perceive what must have been its effect on men born a fallen race, and "whose feet" from infancy had been "swift to shed blood." Accordingly the thrones of that day became filled by kings who were rather monsters than men, and who sported with the lives and happiness of their subjects in the very wantonness of cruelty and injustice.

Now from what quarter, or by what power was this sore evil which lay upon the earth to be either checked or remedied? The principles of stable and equitable government form one of the most complicated of human sciences. None but comprehensive and enlightened minds can fully understand them. The wise and great men who were the fathers of our Republic found the application of them to the wants and welfare of our land, long after they had been tried elsewhere, to be a work which tasked their powers as statesmen to the utmost.

If then, in the midst of the darkness and degradation which were universal throughout the world in the days of old, we find the nation of the Hebrews, yesterday enslaved, feeble and rude, and still struggling with the privations and dangers of the wilderness, yet rising up to our view at once, and showing themselves possessed of laws which secured to them every blessing of civil freedom, which so combined the various powers of the state as equally to secure the rights of the weak and the strong, the poor and the rich; the question arises,—How came this favored people into the possession of enactments ensuring to them a freedom so invaluable in itself, so unknown before their day, and to which the nations around them were still utter strangers? Was it "from heaven or of men?" Was it taught them of God, or did it spring from the then dim wisdom of earth? I ask the statesman, who knows what government is, and the wisdom required to devise it. I ask the historian, who has read history with the eye of philosophy, and who knows what the events of time should teach us. Both, I venture to say, will answer, that such an achievement was as far beyond the wisdom of that day, as the creation of a world lay beyond its power.

Let us then turn at once to the Book in which are recorded the ordinances given to the Hebrews for their government as a nation; and let us see how far it reveals the principles which are essential to civil liberty as displayed in a wisely constructed Republic. Essential, we say, for there are many things in civil polity, when wisely adjusted, which should be left to be regulated by circumstances or considerations of expediency. Such are the number of offices which the laws may embrace; their relations to each other, and the terms on which they are held.

These may be different in one nation from what they are in another, and yet the people themselves may be equally free. In like manner also, a government may be varied so as to meet the various pursuits and interests of different nations, and yet preserve all that enters into a true perception of public freedom. A community that is chiefly employed in commerce, will require laws very different from those adapted to the welfare of a people who expend their main strength in agriculture. But, notwithstanding these diversities in free States, still these are great features which cannot be severed from public liberty without either impairing or destroying it; and these, we say, are all to be found divinely appointed, and brought more or less into action in the commonwealth of the Hebrews. We find here

Government by representation, the election of rulers by the ruled, the public officer chosen by the public voice.—"This," observes the celebrated Chateaubriand, "may be classed among three or four discoveries that have created another universe." The question we would ask is, where, when, and among whom was this great principle first introduced? The great majority of nations are still ignorant of it. There was a time, as we have seen; when it was unknown to all. We ask, what people first brought it into practice and enjoyed the freedom that springs from it?

An accomplished historian of modern times, thinks it can be traced to the early councils of the Christian church.* We believe that a still higher antiquity belongs to it, and that we first meet with it among the Hebrews, when in the wilderness, soon after they were brought out from the bondage of Egypt.

The subject may be said to come before us, but bearing a merely incipient shape, in the advice of Jethro to Moses, when "Israel was encamped at the mount of God." Exodus, 18 : 13–24. "It came to pass on the morrow," as we are told, "that Moses sat to judge the people, and the people stood by Moses from the morning unto the evening." When Jethro had seen how constantly and laboriously Moses was occupied in "judging between one and another" of the people, "when they had a matter;" he wisely said, "the thing that thou doest is not good. Thou will surely wear away, both thou and this people that is with thee; for this thing is too heavy for thee; thou art not able to perform it thyself alone. Hearken now unto my voice, I will give thee counsel, and God shall be with thee: Be thou for the people to God-ward, that thou mayest bring

* Note B.

the causes unto God: and thou shalt teach them ordinances and laws, and shalt show them the way wherein they must walk, and the work that they must do." But having thus advised Moses to restrict himself to the work which properly belonged to him as the inspired teacher and leader of the people, Jethro proceeds with his counsel, saying, "Moreover thou shalt provide out of all the people, able men, such as fear God, men of truth, hating covetousness; and place such over them to be rulers of thousands, and rulers of hundreds, rulers of fifties, and rulers of tens; and let them judge the people at all seasons; and it shall be that every great matter they shall bring unto thee, but every small matter they shall judge. If thou shalt do this thing, and God command thee so, then thou shalt be able to endure, and all this people shall go to their place in peace. So Moses hearkened to the voice of his father-in-law, and did all that he had said."

It is to be observed that no reference is here made to a choice of rulers by the people, either in the advice given by Jethro, or in the action founded upon it. Probably he did not contemplate such a thing. It would seem that this counsel came from a higher source. Jethro was both a wise man and a worshipper of the true God; and feeling that the introduction of such a magistracy as he recommended was a measure of vast importance to the nation, he referred Moses to God for a special intimation of the Divine will, when he should proceed to act in the matter. "If," says he, "thou shalt do this thing, and God shall command thee so," or so authorize and commission thee, as the Hebrew word properly means, thus intimating that the thing was not to be done unless God would command or authorize the proceeding. No one who is acquainted with the close and habitual intercourse which Moses maintained with God, in all that he did as the leader of Israel, can doubt as to his having asked for the Divine direction which Jethro judged so indispensable. And what were the steps which he actually took in order to provide rulers for the people after he had sought instruction from God; he himself tells us in the Book of Deuteronomy, where he recites the whole transaction; and specifies both what the people did, and what he did on the memorable occasion.

We should remember that the name of "Deuteronomy" is given to this Book of the Pentateuch, because it contains a second or supplementary account of what was announced as the law or will of God, on the subjects to which it refers. Let us then look at what Moses here declares to have been done when rulers were appointed; and observe the minuteness with which he pictures out the whole proceedings from first to last. Deut. 1 : 9-18. "I spake unto you at that time, saying, I am not able to bear you myself alone: the Lord your God hath multiplied you, and behold, ye are this day as the stars of heaven for multitude. How can I myself alone bear your cumbrance, and your burden, and your strife?" Having thus alluded to the necessity which called for the appointment of rulers, what does he describe as the first step for the accomplishment of the object? It is "Take you (or select for yourselves)* wise men, and understanding, and known among your tribes, and I will make them rulers over

* הָבוּ· לָכֶם אֲנָשִׁים are the Hebrew words, and they are the same which are used by Joshua, (18 : 4,) where having reproved the children of Israel for allowing seven tribes still to remain without "their inheritance in the land which the Lord God had given them;" he directs, "Give out from among you," or select for yourselves, "three men for each tribe: and I will send them, and they shall rise and go through the land, and describe it into seven parts." It was an important mission on which these men were to be sent, and before they were authorized to proceed upon it they were to be selected, or "given out" by the voice of the people. Many other passages might be cited to show that this is the meaning of the verb הָבוּ· The generic idea is to put forth, to propose, or prefer for some given object: as in 2 Samuel, 11: 15. "Set ye," or put ye forth, "Uriah in the fore-front of the hottest battle;" the post of honor, as it was the post of danger for the brave soldier; and which no doubt Uriah would readily take, little conscious as he was of the treachery by which he was to be sacrificed.

you. And ye answered me, and said, The thing which thou hast spoken is good for us to do. So I took the chief of your tribes, wise men, and known, and made them heads over you, captains over thousands, and captains over hundreds, and captains over fifties, and captains over tens, and officers among your tribes. And I charged your judges at that time, saying, Hear the causes between your brethren, and judge righteously between every man and his brother, and the stranger that is with him. Ye shall not respect persons in judgment; but ye shall hear the small as well as the great; ye shall not be afraid of the face of man; for the judgment is God's: and the cause that is too hard for you, bring it unto me, and I will hear it. And I commanded you at that time all the things that you should do."*

There can be no doubt as to the object in view throughout the transaction here described. It was the creation of a civil magistracy in a form adapted to the existing wants of the people. And we find in the proceedings so carefully and distinctly recited by Moses, the origin or the first precedent of elective civil government. It appears to have been among the first things ordained for the Hebrew nation, after they were brought out from their bondage in Egypt, and were being formed into a State.

* Note C.

It was also one of the great privileges that distinguished them from all other nations of the earth, which still remained under the merciless tyranny already described as the calamity of the human race at that day. And observe, how fully the record covers every essential point in the case.

In the first place, the candidates for office were not to be selected from any one privileged class. They were taken "out of all the people." They must be well known for their intellectual and moral worth, and their fitness for the stations to which they were chosen. They were to be, as it is here expressed, "able men, such as fear God, men of truth, hating covetousness;" "wise men and understanding, and known among the tribes;" and these qualifications being not only all-important but all-sufficient, none others were required.

In the second place, the voice of the people to be ruled was the first step in the appointment of the ruler. It was to "all Israel," that the direction was given, "Take you," or choose for yourselves, "wise men," &c. and it was the people over whom the magistrates were to act, who answered Moses, saying, "The thing which thou hast spoken is good for us to do."

In the third place, after the rulers were thus chosen, they were inducted into office by an appropriate existing authority. Moses, who had his commission direct from Heaven, "made them rulers," as it is here termed; in other words, invested them with the authority to which the people had previously chosen them, and gave them a charge which might well be adopted as a manual by every one who is called to the exercise of civil magistracy.*

Such it seems was the mode in which, by Divine direction, office was conferred in the Hebrew Commonwealth. The government was in every just sense a government of the people. The magistrate was chosen by the suffrages of those among whom he was to act; and at the same time well known integrity and competency were the only qualifications

* In a state of society so simple as that of the Hebrews, when an organized magistracy was first given them, no disadvantage could well arise from having different offices filled by the same man, to an extent that would not be wise or safe for a community in which interests have become more complicated and various. In the passages quoted above we find men described as "Chiefs of the tribes," as "Heads over the people," as "Rulers," as "Captains," as "Officers," and then addressed as "Judges." This latter term, indeed, seems to have been of very extensive application in the Hebrew Commonwealth. It is sometimes applied to those who were employed in the ordinary administration of justice; and again to such as Jepthah, Gideon and others, to whom, as chief magistrates of the nation, were committed the supreme command of the armies and other important trusts. A union of different offices in the same man, or the same body of men, is a thing not unknown in modern governments, our own among the number.

required for any station, from the highest to the lowest. For the same rule indeed seems to have been applied not only to officers chosen for the regular discharge of duties in the Commonwealth, but also to others selected for special occasions. When twelve men were to be selected, to " search out the land," and to point out the way in which the tribes should go up to possess it, the voice of " all Israel " was first heard.* When, seven tribes remaining without their inheritance, three men from each tribe were to be deputed to " go through the land and describe it, and divide it into seven parts;" they were not sent on their mission till first chosen by the people.† When Jepthah was called to take command in the war against the children of Ammon and to be judge over Israel, he assumed no authority till " the people made him head and captain over them."‡ And even when the nation, in their folly and disobedience to God, insisted on having a king over them; the crown, during the first and better ages of the monarchy, seems not to have been worn till the man was made king by the voice of the people, or of their representatives acting in their names. From these and other examples which might be given, it would seem as if every proper occasion had been embraced to give a full and repeated sanction to the

* Deut. 1: 1, 22. † Josh. 18: 3, 4. ‡ Jud. 11: 11.

great principle, that authority, whether ordinary or extraordinary, should emanate from those on whose behalf it was to be employed. After what forms elections may have been conducted; how nearly or remotely resembling those adopted in modern elective governments are inquiries of small moment. They do not affect the position, that the officer held his office from an acknowledged constituency, and that his constituents were those over whom and among whom his authority was exercised.*

* In this connection we may properly advert to the legitimate meaning of the term or phrase, "Congregation of Israel," so frequently mentioned in the history of the Hebrews. No doubt it sometimes means all the people numerically considered; but in many cases it evidently means an assembly acting as representatives of the people. Acts and proceedings are often attributed to "the Congregation," when from the nature of the occasion the whole population could neither have acted nor have been present to act. While on the way to Canaan, and at the time of their entrance into the promised land, the whole population must have amounted to about 2,500,000. Can we suppose this vast multitude to have been meant when it was commanded respecting an offender, "Let all the congregation stone him?" Few questions could arise requiring more nice and careful discrimination than the right of the man-slayer to protection, when he fled to the city of refuge. Can we then suppose the whole people, old and young, to be meant, when it is said, "Then the congregation shall judge between the slayer and the revenger of blood, according to these judgments; and the congregation shall deliver the slayer out of the hand of the revenger of blood, and the congregation shall restore him to the city of his refuge, whither he was fled?" It was

Another great element of civil freedom is a *Judiciary which provides for the prompt and equal administration of justice between man and man.* It has been wisely observed, that "the best laws are those which are best administered;" and if you turn to the ordinances given by God to the Hebrews for carrying the laws of the land into effect, you will find them admirably adapted to their end, giving equal security to the poor and to the rich against violence and wrong.

Their courts of justice were of various grades; some known as High Courts of Appeal; and others so simple and multiplied as to carry the administration of justice to every man's door, and effectually to secure the parties against that ruinous evil, "the law's delay." "Judges and officers shalt thou make

the "wise men," who alone were competent to act in cases of such judicial delicacy and importance. "The Tabernacle of the Congregation" was probably so called because it was the place where the high authorities of the nation held their sittings and deliberations. Such a conventional or technical use of the term corresponds with the meaning which we attribute to words of similar import, as Assembly, Congress, Convention, &c. When we speak of the Assembly of the State of New-York, or of the Congress of the United States, we do not mean the whole numerical population of the State, or of the Nation; but their representatives, chosen to act on their behalf and in their name. The remarks of Michaelis on this subject are so just that I have made an extract from them in Note D.

thee in all thy gates," was the command; and to what a minute subdivision this creation of tribunals was carried out, you see in another ordinance already quoted, directing that there should be "rulers over thousands, rulers over hundreds, rulers over fifties, and rulers over tens, who should judge the people at all seasons." With a judiciary constructed and ramified after this manner, justice could be administered promptly and freely; and on the other hand, a remedy was provided against the evils of hasty decisions, which could not fail in the end to discover and maintain the right of the case. The different courts to which lay the power of appeal, were so formed as to preclude undue bias, arising from pre-judgment; and as a last or ultimate resort, was the venerable Council of Seventy, who held their sittings in the sanctuary, and combined the choice wisdom of the nation, selected with special reference to their high trust.*

Had I time, I would dwell on those great and essential principles of law and equity, according to which suits were conducted and decisions rendered in all these courts, whether higher or lower. Let me simply add, that according to such profound jurists and scholars as Sir Matthew Hale, Hooker, Blackstone, Sir William Jones, Goguet, Grotius, Michaelis,

* Note E.

and our own Ames, Marshall, Story and Kent, there is not a civilized nation, of either ancient or modern times, which has not borrowed from the laws of Moses whatever is most essential to the administration of justice between man and man, or between nation and nation. The rules of evidence in conducting trials; the principles upon which verdicts should be rendered, both in civil and criminal cases; together with the great institution of Trial by Jury, are all found in greater or less development in the statutes and ordinances given from God to the Hebrews; and just in proportion as they are well understood and faithfully carried out, are a community safe in their rights, whether of person or of property.

There is still another prominent feature of the Hebrew commonwealth, which we will briefly notice. *We here see different tribes so confederated as to form one nation.* Such a confederacy, we are told by accomplished statesmen, is of essential importance to the stability and strength of a republic embracing either a numerous population or an extensive territory. In the republics of Italy, as Venice and others, we see the evils resulting from the want of this federative bond; and we have examples of its happy influence in the United Netherlands, and more especially among ourselves in America. The original model for it, you find among the Hebrews.

Among them, the twelve tribes might fitly be called the Twelve United States, united under one general government, by a confederacy which rendered the nation at large the only legitimate authority for purposes of general welfare. But on the other hand, a careful examination of their polity and history will show that the tribes were not so absorbed by the national confederacy, as to lose their character of distinct States or communities. They maintained within themselves such an organization as furnished the most effective safeguards against that centralization of power, which has sometimes rendered civil freedom an easy prey to a daring usurper, or cost rivers of blood to defeat his purposes.

Here it should be added, that these great elements of freedom which we have enumerated, as ordained for the Hebrews, were embodied in a *written Constitution.* No nation can expect to preserve its civil privileges unless they are secured and perpetuated in a record which both rulers and ruled can read, to which both can refer, and which is binding on both. Accordingly it was enjoined on Joshua, and others who succeeded him in authority, that they should "observe to do according to all that was written in the Book of the Law." Had the enactments promising liberty, safety and justice to the people, been left to be handed down by oral tradition or testimony, they would soon have become changed, as the will of ambitious or designing rulers might have dictated. But here they were rendered stable and permanent in a code which might be called the Magna Charta of the Hebrew State.

Such were the essential and leading principles of civil freedom in the Hebrew commonwealth; and their happy influence was felt in the nation during the long period of four hundred years. The system, as a distinct form of government, was introduced by Moses at the Mount of Horeb, and lasted during his life, the life of Joshua, and the lives of others, who successively "judged Israel," until it was superseded by the introduction of monarchy in the days of Saul. During these four centuries events of paramount importance transpired. The whole economy of Old Testament worship was ordained and brought into general observance, the people were led through the wilderness and established in the land promised to their fathers, and their name became feared and respected by surrounding nations. A succession of men were raised up so renowned that their names are commemorated and embalmed in the New Testament, for their wisdom, their courage, and their piety. "What shall I more say?" says Paul, "for the time would fail me to tell you of Gideon, and of Barak, and of Samson, and of Jephthah, of David also, of Samuel and the prophets: who through faith subdued kingdoms, wrought righteousness, obtained promises, stopped the mouths of lions, quenched the violence of fire, escaped the edge of the sword; out of weakness were made strong, waxed valiant in fight, turned to flight the armies of the aliens." The condition of the nation during this period, is several times referred to in their subsequent history as pre-eminently distinguished for the faithful respect shown to the ordinances of religion, and for the general prevalence of prosperity in the land. However great may have been the zeal and liberality of Josiah for restoring and observing the passover after it had been long neglected, the utmost that could be said of the occasion was, "surely there was not holden such a passover from the days of the judges that judged Israel, nor in all the days of the kings of Israel, or of the kings of Judah." And when David receives assurance of future prosperity to the nation, it is described to be such as prevailed when God "commanded judges to be over his people Israel." The calamities that befël the commonwealth were often occasioned by their neglect to maintain the government in its entireness, which God had prescribed for them; and in every instance their suffering and degradation are shown to be in consequence of "their turning away from the Lord," in order to demonstrate by a repeated and convincing record, that no people can have civil freedom without true religion; and that where they cease to serve and honor the Most High, they prepare the way for anarchy within, and for defeat and oppression from without. Indeed to impress that truth on the nations of the earth, seems to have been one great end for which the "Book of Judges" was written.*

From the view we have taken of the principles embodied in the civil Constitution of the Hebrews, we see

1. The error of supposing the Government to have been a pure Theocracy. It was a Theocracy only in a limited sense. Every reader of their history must know that the Hebrews had, like other nations, their civil rulers, men who exercised authority over other men, and who were acknowledged throughout the land as its rightful magistrates. While, then, we admit that the Most High, on fitting occasions, claimed to be the lawgiver, judge and ruler of Israel, in a sense peculiar to himself; we hold itto have been a part of his divine legislation to frame the enactments which show how civil authority of man over man should be created, and how it should be administered so as best to promote the welfare of a people.

* Note F.

2. Observe the wisdom displayed in the brevity, simplicity, and comprehensiveness of the framework here ordained for the government of the nation. The three great principles which we have found in their polity, are: (1.) Election of the rulers by the ruled: (2.) A judiciary wisely constructed for the speedy and safe administration of justice: And, (3.) A union of the tribes under a confederation, well adapted to be a safeguard against usurpation from within, and to afford protection against invasion from without. The wisdom and mercy which fixed these great landmarks of human rights and civil freedom, left it to man to draw them out into different forms, and with different applications, as the various wants and circumstances of different nations might require. In this way, indeed, all the elementary principles of law and justice are revealed in the Bible. God never legislates too much, or too little. He leaves scope for the study and labors of the wise and the good; and, at the same time, establishes by his express authority, those great boundary lines of truth and right which may hem in the mind from capital error.

3. We see what was the sin of the people in "asking for a king," "that they might be like all the nations, and that their king might judge them, and go out before them and fight their battles." There is no doubt that there was much sin in the demand.

While Samuel was told to comply with their wishes, he was directed to do it under "solemn protest;" nor was their first king well proclaimed till they themselves made the confession, "we have added to all our sins this evil, to ask us a king." "I gave thee a king in mine anger," said God to the nation; for in his wise and mysterious providence he often makes the gratification of a sinful desire a punishment for having indulged it. But wherein lay the sinfulness of the nation in demanding "a king to reign over them?" Not in their having overturned the theocracy by their wilfulness. The theocracy remained as entire under Saul and David, as it had been under Moses or Joshua. Their guilt is described in the words of God to Samuel: "They have not rejected thee, but they have rejected me, that I should not reign over them." To reject God, or to refuse to have him reign over us, is the scriptural language for rejecting or putting dishonor on his ordinances and commandments; and the sin of asking for a king, lay in their rejecting the government which God had provided for them as a nation, which ensured to them the blessings of Civil Freedom; and in choosing another which subjected them to the evils that were the burden and calamity of the kingdoms around them. Accordingly, Samuel is directed to add to his protest against their choice, a description of "the manner of the king that should reign over them," depicting the tyranny which they were about to bring upon themselves, in true and faithful colors. "He will take your sons," said the prophet, "and appoint them for himself, for his chariots, and to be his horsemen; and some shall run before his chariots. And he will appoint him captains over thousands, and captains over fifties; and will set them to ear his ground, and to reap his harvest, and to make his instruments of war, and instruments of his chariots. And he will take your daughters to be confectionaries, and to be cooks, and to be bakers. And he will take your fields, and your vineyards, and your olive-yards, even the best of them, and give them to his servants." They were smitten with a lust for the trappings and pomp of royalty; and they persisted in their demand for it, though it would result, as they were here told, in the wanton violation of their domestic enjoyments and private rights, and in the surrender of themselves, and of all that they now called their own, to the will of the monarch; while, in order to obtain their sinful wish, they threw away a government simple in its form, imposing no heavy burdens on the people for its support, and preserving that constant sympathy between the ruler and the ruled which can result only from his being one of themselves, and chosen by them to his authority over them. True, the fatal reverse was not felt all at once. Corruptions of justice, and the encroachments of tyranny are always gradually developed in a nation. It requires time for them to grow. But the root of the tree which produced such bitter fruit was planted among the Hebrews when they asked and obtained "a king to rule over them."

4. The theory we have been explaining serves to show how, and on what principle resistance to rulers becomes lawful and even dutiful. This is a question which has excited earnest and bitter controversy. When civil liberty was making some of her most important advances in England, "the right divine of kings to govern wrong" was advocated with unblushing assurance.* Filmer wrote his Patriarcha to show that no degree of injustice or oppression, on the part of the throne, can justify resistance on the part of the subject. Locke brought his powerful mind to overthrow this preposterous doctrine of passive obedience and non-resistance; but in his Treatise on Civil Government he introduced his theory of a Social Compact between rulers and ruled, in which he would have the duty of obedience to rest in a voluntary consent previously given. Later writers have objected to this view of the case, because such a compact must be in a great degree

* Note G.

imaginary. We avoid the difficulty, and can, at the same time, learn how the subjects of a government may lawfully withstand oppression, if we turn to the Bible. It does not teach that the mere possession of power so renders it the ordinance of God, that it should in no case be resisted.* On the contrary, much as the sentiment may have been misrepresented, resistance to tyrants is sometimes obedience to God. By his ordinance, as we have seen, civil authority is made a trust from the ruled to the rulers; a trust committed to those who hold it, for a specified object, "for the punishment of evil doers, and the praise of them that do well." Of course, authority being of the nature of a trust, may be so perverted and abused as to annul its own claims to submission. The best, and the true mode of conveying this trust, is by the election of their rulers by the people themselves. In this way, they will generally retain in their own hands the most effectual security against continued wrong or oppression; for they can redress themselves by a change of rulers, without recourse to violence. But if, through folly or misfortune, a people are destitute of this advantage, still, civil authority is not the less a trust, according to the appointment of God. And if it becomes so abused as to effect the injury and not the benefit of the ruled, in such case

* Note H.

the end of the Most High in ordaining government, is defeated by those who were entrusted with it; and a people should feel it to be alike their privilege and their duty to resist such oppression, and to obtain redress by such means as may be in their power. And here will arise a question that can always be most safely decided when the occasion arrives that calls for the decision. How far Government must be perverted from its legitimate object before it ceases to have farther claims to allegiance, or at what point of oppression resistance becomes either wise or dutiful, forms an inquiry which must be left to the exercise of a sound wisdom seeking direction, from both the word and the providence of God. There may be circumstances in which wisdom and duty would lead us to endure rather than to resist, long after civil government has become oppressive, and has lost all just claim to obedience. Resistance without the rational prospect of relief would only add to the evil instead of bringing redress. The fathers of our Republic justified their revolt from the authority of the British crown, on the principle that there should be no taxation without representation. To submit to the former, without possessing the latter, they considered as opening the door to every species of unrighteous exaction. But when they had settled the great point, that resistance was right in the sight of God, they also looked to their means of resisting successfully. The result showed the wisdom of their deliberations. Had they failed to achieve our independence, their recourse to arms would have been accounted treason, and they must have paid the penalty with their lives. They prevailed; and the Revolution they effected has been followed by the formation of a Republic which is now a study for the nations of the earth.

5. From the view we have taken of the Hebrew Government, we cannot fail to perceive its great superiority over that of other ancient nations, however distinguished for their love of freedom. I would be far from undervaluing the sages whose names brighten the pages of Greek and Roman history. According to the light they enjoyed, they did much that redounds to their praise. They have left behind them sentiments of lofty patriotism which should never be forgotten. But they had not the knowledge that could enable them to adjust the delicate framework of national government, so as to ensure efficiency and stability to the authorities, and yet secure the rights of the people from violation. Perhaps no one ever exceeded Milton in his relish for all that belongs to the wisdom and refinement of Greece and Rome; and yet, when he speaks of their wise men, as legislators, he describes them as

"Statists indeed;
And lovers of their country, as may seem;
But herein to our prophets, far beneath,
As men divinely taught, and better teaching
The solid rules of civil government,
In their majestic, unaffected style,
Than all the oratory of Greece and Rome.
In them is plainest taught, and easiest learnt,
What makes a nation happy, and keeps it so."

As we endeavor to show in another place, there is nothing in which the Greeks and Romans were distinguished from other Pagan nations, be it "in science or in song," for which they are not more or less indebted to the heaven-taught Hebrews; the best achievements of the one being sometimes but imperfect copies of models found with the other. In nothing is this inferiority more plainly seen than in their legislation and their laws for insuring equal and just freedom to the whole people. At the very time when Rome was boasting loudly of her liberty, the people, who formed the great mass of the Commonwealth, were, as a class, studiously excluded from the high places of power and emolument; such privileges being reserved for those who could boast of Patrician blood and Patrician wealth. Under the Hebrew Constitution, the candidate for office might be rich or poor, descended from an ancestry either known or unknown; if he was an "able man, loving truth, and hating covetousness, and known among the tribes" to possess these qualifications, he might aspire to the highest office in the State. In the right of suffrage, there was as much difference as we find in the qualifications of the candidates. Among the Hebrews, those who shared in the public burdens had a voice in the election of the public officer. In Rome, those who bore the heaviest part of the burdens of the State had generally the least influence in deciding who should administer the Government. The tribunals for the administration of justice gave farther evidence of the superiority of the Hebrew Constitution. It provided every reasonable security that "the small as well as the great might be heard," and equal justice awarded them. Under the Roman Judiciary a wide door for corruption was left open, rendering the poor and the weak easy victims to the rich and the strong.

6. In this connection, I observe that a careful examination of all Republics, whether ancient or modern, will serve to show that none of them embrace so fully the great principles of Civil Freedom revealed in the Bible as the United States of America. The Fathers of our Republic may not themselves have been aware of the close resemblance between the cardinal features of the Constitution which they framed for us, as a nation, and those

which we have seen revealed through the Hebrew lawgiver. If so, it is only another proof that the destinies of our land have always been under auspices better and safer than could have sprung from human wisdom and human power.

But as points like these which I have briefly mentioned have been ably discussed by men who have made the science of Government their special study, I pass on to notice another feature in the laws of the Hebrew Commonwealth which seems not to be so well understood.

In our day, we hear much concerning the empire of public opinion. It is the best and safest of all human empires. It is the empire of mind instead of brute force, and will always prevail when intelligence is generally diffused, and thought is free and untrammelled. Mere statute law is comparatively powerless, if public opinion is against it. Civil liberty, too, even if achieved to-day, may be lost to-morrow, unless there is accompanying it a sound public opinion growing out of general intelligence, and an elevated tone of moral sentiment among the mass of a people. Hence the great importance of those regulations in a community which tend to improve the standard of public sentiment. Perhaps at the time when they are working out their effect on the character of a nation, their influence may be so gradual and silent as not to be perceived. But every wise observer must know that causes which go to form public opinion, like the drops of rain, though of small account when taken separately, yet lead to immense results when acting in their aggregate power. In this view of them, you find the wisdom of many laws given to the Hebrews, some of which might otherwise appear strange, if not ludicrous.

We should remember that previous to the time of which we are now speaking, the Hebrews had been an enslaved, and, in many respects, a degraded people. To meet their case, and to promote their improvement in mind and manners, the Most High not only ordained for them a system of intellectual training, which we will hereafter consider, but he also gave them laws like the following:—

"If a bird's nest chance to be before thee in the way, in any tree or on the ground, and the dam sitting upon the young or upon the eggs, thou shalt not take the dam with the young: but thou shalt in any wise let the dam go, and take the young to thee, that it may be well with thee, and that thou mayest prolong thy days." It should be observed that the reason annexed to this statute is the same which we find added to the fifth command of the Decalogue, "Honor thy father and thy mother."

The argument used to enforce both the precepts, is, "that it may be well with thee, and that thou mayest prolong thy days;" thus showing that there must be some intimate connection between the two. And if any of us have seen the distress of a bird, "the dam," when her nest is rifled of her young, her maternal tenderness rendering her an easy prey as she rushes within the grasp of the spoiler; you can see the beautiful moral to be found in the law forbidding the Hebrew to take "the dam" when he is carrying away her young from the nest; and how it bears on the obedience to be rendered to the command, "Honor thy father and thy mother." It was designed to cultivate a high regard for parental feeling. No advantage must be taken of it, says God; it must always be treated with a tender respect, though it be the maternal anxiety of a bird of the air when distressed for her offspring.

A man who can sport with parental sympathy gives sure proof of a hard and corrupted heart. We can all remember how we have abhorred the tyrant Gessler in the unnatural task which he laid on the patriot William Tell. The hero was required as the ransom for his own life, to place an apple on the head of his son; and then standing at the utmost distance of a bowshot, to cleave the apple in two

*Note I.

with an arrow. The feat was performed; and when Gessler perceived that another arrow remained in the hand of the father, and inquired for what purpose it was intended, he was told, "Sir, the second arrow was for your heart, if the first had even touched my dear boy." And had this been the issue, few would have mourned the fate of the tyrant after he had thus wantonly outraged the affection of a father.

There is a wrong mode of doing even that which is right and which may convert it into a positive evil. Charity is sometimes bestowed on the poor with a manner that renders the gift not only offensive in the sight of God, but a source of more bitter pain to the receiver than the pinchings of want. To cherish a suitable and right spirit in deeds of benevolence, it was commanded, "When ye reap the harvest of your land, thou shalt not wholly reap the corn out of thy field, neither shalt thou gather the gleanings of thy harvest. And thou shalt not glean thy vineyards, neither shalt thou gather every grape of the vineyard; thou shalt leave them for the poor and the stranger. I am the Lord your God." This precept was to remind the Hebrews, that the poor should be allowed to share in the comforts as well as in the absolute necessaries of life, inasmuch as a share in the produce of both the "vineyard" and "field" must be allowed to them; and that, as poverty has its feelings of delicacy as well as wealth, instead of obliging the destitute to come and confess to us their need, and receive alms at our hands and in our sight, they should be allowed the opportunity of gaining relief when no eye would be upon them but the eye of God, and, in a way that seemed to render it in part the reward of their own labor.

In close alliance with this, is another commandment. "No man shall take the upper or the nether mill-stone to pledge; for he taketh a man's life to pledge." Here the principle is established which is recognized in all civilized and Christian nations, that a man cannot be deprived of a necessary means of sustaining life for himself and his family, by distraint for debt. But see also what is added as to pledges that might be taken for payment. "When thou dost lend thy brother any thing, thou shalt not go into his house to fetch his pledge; thou shalt stand abroad, and the man to whom thou dost lend, shall bring out the pledge abroad unto thee." Want must have been sorely felt before a man will pledge that which properly belongs to, and forms a part of his home. Hence the Hebrew was told, you must not go into his house, to pain his feelings and the feelings of his family, by witnessing the tokens of their destitution, or the distress they may suffer at parting with some long possessed and much valued article of their furniture. No, said the law, you must stand without, till the man bring abroad to thee whatever is pledged, that the hardship may be as little felt as the nature of the case will admit.

Again, it is ordained, "Thou shalt not oppress a hired servant that is poor and needy, whether he be of thy brethren, or of the strangers that are within thy gates. At his day thou shalt give him his hire, neither shall the sun go down upon it, for he is poor and setteth his heart upon it." There is a principle of mingled kindness and justice involved in this ordinance, which many masters in our day would do well to remember. Too often are the feelings of servants exasperated, and their interests made to suffer, not by ultimately wronging them out of their wages, but by vexatious delays to pay them what has been earned by their faithful labor. To induce the master both to respect the anxieties, and satisfy the just claims of his servant, it is here commanded, "At his day thou shalt give him his hire, for he setteth his heart upon it."

To give a few more examples: it furnishes certain evidence of high moral sentiment, and is a most efficient means of promoting it, when all classes in a community evince due respect for age. Hence the command, "Thou shalt rise up before the hoary head, and honor the face of the old man, and fear thy

God." Not only justice, but kindness to a stranger, showing both a sympathy for his feelings and a due regard for his rights, is another of those proprieties of life which denote the same cultivated spirit in a people. Accordingly it was enjoined, "Ye shall neither vex a stranger nor oppress him; for ye know the heart of a stranger, seeing ye were strangers in the land of Egypt." A disposition to ridicule or take advantage of those who are deformed, or labor under some bodily infirmity, both shows and produces coarseness of mind and hardness of heart. Hence the command, "Thou shalt not curse the deaf, nor put a stumbling-block before the blind: but shalt fear thy God." To be in the habit of approaching falsehood, though not actually committing the crime, must inevitably destroy a nice and proper sense of truth, and in the end bring the mind to the actual commission of what had thus become familiar to its view. Accordingly it was commanded, "Thou shalt not raise a false report—keep thee far from a false matter."

These are some of the statutes by which the national mind in the Hebrew Commonwealth was trained to a high standard of public sentiment; imparting to all classes a sensibility to the proprieties of life, and a spontaneous regard to its relative duties, which, in some degree, render a people a law unto themselves. To produce and perpetuate such a governing power, the power of opinion, is the very essence of wise legislation; and in proportion to its strength and prevelance among a people, will the foundations of civil freedom be strong and enduring.

In the view of our subject, thus spread before you, we observe,

As the Bible contains the origin of civil liberty, by the Bible alone can it be sustained. The law seems to be of general application, that wherever we find the source of existence, there also we find the aliment of growth and strength. It is so with the herb of the field, with man himself, and with every blessing he enjoys, whether personal or social, civil or religious. What we may infer from the analogy of the case, we are taught by the evidence of facts—facts of ancient and of modern times, gathered from every quarter of the globe where freedom either still holds her blessed sway, or, after struggling for existence, has finally perished. It is the decree of Him who has ordained that light shall shine from the sun, that liberty and the Bible shall always be found united: and "what God hath joined together let not man put asunder." There can be no divorce from this union. If the Bible goes, liberty follows. How was it in the land of the Hebrews?

When the Most High gave them civil freedom, he gave them also the Bible of that day with it; and when they abandoned or neglected the one, they lost the other also. In the language of their own history, "It was when the law of the Lord was not found" in the hands of magistrates and people that the sun of their prosperity waned, and waned till it went down in darkness and blood.

And how comes it, that in modern times, on our own Continent, at our very doors, we have seen Province after Province throwing off the yoke of foreign dominion; and yet, in their efforts to acquire civil freedom, they "sow to the wind, and reap the whirlwind?" And why, still farther, has the experiment been so successful with us as a nation, which has been so fruitless, or rather so disastrous with them? It is because ours is a land of Bibles, and theirs is not; because here the Holy Book is in the hands of the high and the low, the rich and the poor, swaying, elevating and purifying public sentiment in minds, even where it does not sanctify the heart; and there its pages are sealed to the eyes of the people, and they are left sunk in the pollution and gloom from which no other power but this "light shining in a dark place" can redeem them.

Let the Bible go through the world, as it is yet to go, and it will show itself equally powerful to regenerate the hearts of sinful men, and the spirit of degraded nations. Already, in this day of holy zeal for its spread, it has been carried very far into the regions of Pagan darkness; and in every place where it has quickened into life souls that "were dead in trespasses and sins," it has created also a new dwelling-place for freedom; till the earth is now bespangled with miniature republics, as the sky with stars; and which are yet to spread and widen till every form of tyranny shall crumble before them. But, on the other hand, while this blessing shall be sent to lands now destitute of it, if those who already possess it allow the streams of corruption to spread within their borders, which always follow the disbelief and neglect of the sacred volume, then is their glory departed; and they too must be added to the nations whose names are written in the dust. "The wages of sin is death," says the oracle of God; and it is equally true, whether it be the sin of a man, or the sin of a people. You find the monuments of the sad truth in every age, and in every region of the world. For, go where you will, search where you will on the face of this wide earth, you are treading on the sepulchres not only of men but of nations; nations that once were in their glory, but now are numbered among the lost.

And what can be that worse than lethiferous

wand that has destroyed, by its touch, empire after empire, state after state, till the earth has become thus filled and strewed with their fragments? Is it time that has done it all? Time! what is time? Time has no power of its own; and even with all the aid it can gain from earth, air or sea to make war upon man, or his works, it can spread no ravages that man, if faithful to himself, is unable to repair. No! no! It was not time that buried Babylon and her proud towers so deep in the earth, that scarce a remnant is left to show where once she stood. It was not time that prostrated the lofty columns, the triumphant arches, and vast temples of Roman grandeur and power. Far, very far from it. It was the moral corruption of the people; it was the mocking guilt of man against the God that made him, which has thus desolated kingdoms and nations, till the strongest and mightiest have passed away as "a dream when one awaketh." The story of the cities of the plain is the story of them all from that day onward. Their "iniquity was pride, fulness of bread, and abundance of idleness: neither did they strengthen the hand of the poor and needy;" and "because their sin was very grievous and the cry of it had gone up to Heaven," He rained down upon them a desolation that has engulphed them in its abyss to this day. And whether it be kingdoms or commonwealths, in the old world or in the new, if they become corrupt, emptied of piety towards God and righteousness towards man, they have in their hands "the cup of trembling," which will in the end become to them the cup of death. With every nation that turns away from truth and from right the future is plain to our eyes as the past.

My hearers: it then requires no "hand-writing on the walls" of this Capitol to announce what lies before our now privileged nation. It is revealed in letters of light, and so plainly that "he who runs may read." And what, let me ask, are "the signs of the times" which are to be seen in the skies that overspread our land? Are they portentous of evil, or do they promise good? That clouds are visible, many will admit. But clouds are not always the harbingers of harm. Do the clouds we see rising, threaten a coming tempest that will spread desolation; or do they bear in their bosom the refreshing shower, and when passing away are they to be followed by a new bow of promise? It all centers here. We can hope to be a happy nation, a free nation, only so long as we are a Christian nation. Let this Bible be abandoned by our people; especially let it be shut out from the hearts and counsels of our rulers; and if these noble halls are not profaned by the ruthless hand of some Vandal conqueror, they may be stained by the blood of civil strife, in which the hand of brother is turned against brother. But so long as the Holy Book shall be held in high honor in our Houses of Legislation, our Cabinet Councils, and our Courts of Justice, the nation, with all that forms her real glory, is safe; the ark of the covenant is still with her, and she stands strong against every foe, for she stands in the strength of God. In every crisis which marks her history, she will be found to possess a sustaining and redeeming power, that will carry her triumphantly through; and whether the storms that beat upon the towers of her strength may arise from dissensions within or invasions from without, she will find protection and peace "under the shadow of his wings," who alike "stilleth the noise of the seas, the noise of their waves, and the tumult of the people."

THIRD LECTURE.

"The voice of him that crieth in the wilderness, prepare ye the way of the Lord, make straight in the desert a highway for our God. Every valley shall be exalted, and every mountain and hill shall be made low; and the crooked shall be made straight, and the rough places plain; and the glory of the Lord shall be revealed, and all flesh shall see it together: for the mouth of the Lord hath spoken it." The spirit and beauty of the language well befit the importance of the truth it was designed to convey. Its primary reference is to the advent of the Redeemer, and to the preparation which was made for his coming and for his work, under the ministry of his forerunner John the Baptist. But "to prepare his way" so that his wisdom and goodness might be clearly revealed in the preparation he makes, has been a uniform rule of his procedure in all the great revolutions which he produces in the affairs of men. In the various works of his hands, he is a careful observer of his own laws. He acts through means adequate to their end. He does everything in its season, calls it forth in its due order and connexion.

He gives "first the blade, then the ear, then the full corn in the ear." Thus growth, as he produces it, is healthful and enduring; whether it be growth in man or in the mind of man; whether growth in nations, or in any of those attainments which add to their strength and prosperity. With him, a wise preparation is the first step leading to a happy consummation.

How widely different from this do we often find the designs and efforts of men! They would have the ripe corn, when they should scarcely expect the blade. They demand the vigor and maturity of manhood when there has not been time for a healthful growth from infancy to youth. Many an excellent object of benevolence has been defeated and lost by bringing it forward out of season, and urging it beyond measure. New wine has been put into old bottles, and the bottles have burst, and both have been destroyed. This inconsiderate haste, this "plucking at the pear before it is ripe" is one of the prevailing evils of our age, and involves inquiries which ought to be well examined both by "the leaders of thought and the rulers of men." Unless correct and rational views are entertained on the subject, every device for the amelioration of our race, and especially for their political advantage or advancement, must be perpetually at fault. A nation, like an individual, needs education and time to prepare them for self-government. Many old associations must be broken up, and new associations formed; the popular mind must be trained to new conceptions, new channels of thought, and new standards of right, before men can appreciate the value, understand the responsibilities or discharge the duties of civil freedom. If they grasp after it without such a preparation for it, they are grasping after a shadow, or what may be worse. Their freedom "falsely so called," will degenerate into anarchy and profligacy, from which they will perhaps seek refuge by again submitting to a hardened despotism, as the least of two evils. Accordingly, when God gave the Hebrews a revelation of his will, which established a new platform for the action of rulers and ruled, he prepared the nation for enjoying and preserving the privileges he bestowed on them, by means to which we will now invite your attention.

The first of these preparatory steps was to order *their migration to another country, their departure from Egypt and their settlement in Palestine.* Let us look with some care at the importance which the word and the providence of God assign to this point, migration, or change of abode, when he is about to elevate the moral and intellectual condition of a people. We may here find a striking parallel between the history of the Hebrew nation and of our own.

Enlightened physiologists very generally teach, that, to a great extent, all the varieties of life, whether in the vegetable or animal world, are improved by a change of place, by being transferred to a new region and a new atmosphere. Races or families of plants have been known to become extinct from being kept too long in the same soil; the shepherd has seen his flock pine away from the want of a new pasture ground; and how the bodies of men are invigorated by like changes, is an every-day observation. But I would now speak more directly as to the effect of migration on the moral and mental condition of a people.

We all know something as to the influence of local associations. They not only shape our tastes and desires, but they also have at times a most controlling power to warp and pervert the mind. We may have seen the plant or the tree taking root in the cleft, or on the side of a rock. It is often made to grow out of shape from the circumstances of its situation. As it rises it is met by some projecting crag, or it is bent down by some overhanging fragment, around which it grows, and thus is distorted from its natural form and beauty. So is it with the human mind. It is influenced and directed by surrounding circumstances. Its opinions are often formed so as to accommodate themselves to long existing evils; and, like the tree, grasping and adhering to the point of rock that had marred the beauty of its growth; so also will the mind often embrace and cling to the very errors and wrongs which had deformed and depressed it.

Would you remedy this, you must do with the man as you would with the herb or the tree. You must transplant them both to another soil. You must break up old associations. You must free the man from his familiar and habitual contact with long existing abuses, and enable him to view them at such a distance as to comprehend their magnitude and deformity. Paths of thought can become so beaten, and the mind so worn into them, that it can see nothing beyond them; and if you would give a man new and improved views, you must take him where he can overlook the barriers that once confined his vision. The freshness, the vigor, the elastic spring which are imparted by such a change to the mind and the character, whether of a man or a people, are the result of those great laws by which the Most High governs life in all its forms.

Now observe how uniformly he respects this principle in his most conspicuous movements for the instruction and improvement of man as a rational and immortal being. There are two great periods in Old Testament times, when he was pleased to make special revelations of his will for this end. The first was at the call of Abraham, the commencement of what is styled the Patriarchal dispensation; during which the oracles of God, and the ordinances of his worship were known and preserved in the family of that patriarch. And what was the first command which God laid on Abraham when he was about to elevate him in knowledge and religion above all around him? It was, "Get thee out of thy country, and from thy kindred, and from thy father's house, unto a land that I will show thee: And I will make of thee a great nation, and I will bless thee, and make thy name great; and thou shalt be a blessing." He had hitherto dwelt in Ur of the Chaldees, a chief seat of the idolatries and other evil practices of that ancient people; and now when he was about to become a new man, and to acquire a new name, he is directed at once to seek a new home. And to this do we find Prophets and Apostles afterwards referring as the first step which led to his subsequent greatness as "the friend of God," and the "Father of the Faithful."

When the Mosaic dispensation was made to succeed the Patriarchal, a still farther impulse was given to the cause of knowledge and righteousness in the world by new revelations from God, showing more clearly than ever, the way of salvation through a Redeemer; and giving to the great principles of moral law the form and extent which they retain to this day. It was an era of vast magnitude in the condition and history of the human race, when the "two tables of stone," inscribed with the Decalogue, were given from Sinai, followed by the institutions which were "the example and shadow of heavenly things." From that day forward men began to enjoy "a better hope" towards God, and to feel new responsibilities in all their relations to each other, whether domestic, civil or religious. Accordingly, when God was about to render the Hebrews the depositaries of this world-enriching and world-reforming knowledge, he led them, as he had before led Abraham, from their former abode, and transferred them to a new country; a country where all was new to them; a new soil, new scenery, a new atmosphere; in one sense, a new heaven and a new earth; where new vigor might be imparted to both mind and body for the more perfect discharge of their newly revealed duties to God and to man.

Passing by other examples showing the influence of migration, and which occur in the history of the church and of the world, let us look more carefully at the removal of the Hebrews into the land promised to their fathers, and we shall find still farther designs of wisdom and mercy in it. It would have been migration to a new home, had God led them from Egypt to India or China. Indeed there were countries on every side, where all would have been as new to them as in the land of Canaan. We ask then, was there anything in the character or situation of this land, which rendered it better adapted than others to display his designs of mercy to the nation, and through them to the world at large?

We would naturally suppose there was some good reason for the selection, if we reflect upon the manner in which it was promised to Abraham as the future abode of his descendants, when they should be multiplied into a great nation. It seems in that day to have been the Paradise of the world. It is repeatedly named, as a "land flowing with milk and honey," an expression describing not only extraordinary fertility, but also fertility in everything which contributes to either the health or enjoyments of man. "I am come down," says God, "to deliver my people, and to bring them up out of the land of Egypt, into a good land, and a large, unto a land flowing with milk and honey." We have a still more full description of it, when Moses tells the people, then near the end of their journeyings in the wilderness; "For the Lord thy God bringeth thee into a good land, a land of brooks of water, of fountains and depths that spring out of valleys and hills; a land of wheat, and barley, and vines, and fig trees, and pomegranates; a land of oil olive and honey; a land wherein thou shalt eat bread without scarceness, thou shalt not lack anything in it; a land whose stones are iron, and out of whose hills thou mayest dig brass."

How far these promises of unparalleled fertility were realized, we learn from the teeming millions of inhabitants which the land sustained when the nation had full and undisturbed possession of it. But multitudes are not always strength, and we have but to glance at the descriptions given of it, in order to see how peculiarly the distinguishing features of the country were adapted to elicit those powers and faculties of body and mind which are the best strength and glory of a nation.

Productive labor, and especially labor which draws from the earth her abundant stores, is not only the great source of national wealth, but also a great means of spreading physical and moral health through the mass of a people. The land of the Hebrews yielded comparatively little as spontaneous growth; but responded most bountifully to the labor of industry, especially the industry of the husbandman. It was not like the plains of other climes where the earth of its own accord does so much that the inhabitants need do nothing ; and where every power of the man becomes torpid and feeble through inaction. But to render it fruitful, it was to be tilled and cultivated, the abundance of its returns depending on the abundance and faithfulness of the labor bestowed, a land best of all others adapted to impart a spirit of activity, vigor, sagacity and independence to the inhabitants.

Still more ; no observer of human nature can question the influence of surrounding scenery on the intellect of a people, especially of the more intellectual classes. This was not overlooked by the Most High when he removed the Hebrews to their new home. It was then a part of his design to enlarge the boundaries of human knowledge, to give new revelations of wisdom through his prophets; and he kindled within them the soul of eloquence and song, that the truths which they were sent to teach might be clothed in the rich and glowing language, and illustrated by the splendid and expressive imagery, which all future ages might feel and understand. Accordingly he planted the Hebrews amid scenery of such mingled beauty and sublimity as might well impart a higher elevation and tone to every faculty of the mind. Judging from the very face of the chosen land, it was just the place in which the writers of the Bible ought to have lived; for it furnished those materials of thought and promptings of the heart that could have been found no where else. Even when its palmy days were past, a heathen writer calls it, "a land of charms and graces;" and long as it has been trodden down and defaced by Saracen and Turk, travellers tell us that in its rich and varied beauties, though like beauty in a shroud, it is still what the Prophet has called it, "the glory of all lands."

As another advantage, we might allude to the natural barriers which surrounded it as a protection against hostile invasion. On every side it was enclosed by seas, by mountains, or by deserts. But we hasten to look at

Its geographical position in reference to the other countries of the whole eastern hemisphere, and to observe how admirable were its local advantages for becoming the central point of illumination to them all; a fountain whence streams of knowledge might flnow, with most ease and rapidity, to a benighted world. "From the wilderness and this Lebanon, even unto the great river, the river Euphrates, and unto the great sea toward the going down of the sun, shall be your coast," says God, when describing the boundaries of the Promised Land. Its western border was the head waters of the Mediterranean, furnishing access to the whole southern coast of Europe, and the whole northern coast of Africa; on the eastern border was the Euphrates, which emptied into the Indian Ocean, and thus opened their way to the whole southern coast of Asia. The design of the Most High in giving the Hebrews this commanding position, rendering them so like "a city set upon a hill," is perhaps too much overlooked. They were far from being an insulated people, unknown and unfelt by other kingdoms of the world. So widely had their fame spread in the reign of Solomon, that not only the Queen of Sheba, "with a very great company," but "all the kings of the earth," as we are told, "sought his presence to hear his wisdom" and become instructed in the laws and ordinances which he so prosperously administered. Jerusalem was more than the Athens of its day. The richest store-house of knowledge for the world was then in the hands of the Hebrews, and from them other nations were ambitious to be learners. To accord with this design respecting them, God fixed their abode. As he set up their laws and institutions for the study of other nations, he planted them in a country so central, that all might have ready access to it, and that the wisdom they possessed from him, might be made to flow most readily to every people.

Here also we should add that a time had now come which rendered this influence most seasonable and needful. There are periods in the history of the world, when iniquity becomes so rife that earth can no longer bear it, nor will Heaven consent longer to behold it; and when it must either be wiped away by the unsparing destruction of those who have thus filled up the measure of their iniquity, as was done at the time of the deluge; or there must be some corrective applied which will lessen if not remedy the prevalence of crime. When the Hebrews were planted in Canaan, the iniquity of the Amorites "was now full;" and so was it also with other kingdoms of that day. Corruption in every form reigned without control. Wrong and cruelty among men, and ignorance and impiety towards God, were everywhere spread abroad, until it might again have "repented God that he had made man;" and had it not been for the healing and restraining waters that went forth from the Holy Land, another deluge might have been sent to "destroy man from the face of the earth," and all the inhabited globe been "made like unto Sodom and Gomorrah."

In what forms, and to what extent this reforming influence was felt among surrounding nations, both in that, and in succeeding ages, we will hereafter more fully show. I must, for the present, pass by these and other topics, that I may reserve more room for an application of the subject as already explained, and which every one will admit to be especially seasonable.

The motto in our national ensign, "E Pluribus Unum," seems to have a prophetic meaning perhaps not contemplated by the venerable men who adopted it. We are not only one commonwealth formed out of many states, but we are one people gathered from many nations. The sentiment pervades the civilized world, and we cannot change it if we would, that here is the emigrant's home; that our western hemisphere, and especially our portion of it, is designed to be an asylum for the oppressed of the eastern; and that races of the human family which there have become worn out and effete, are here to be restored by a new growth. Such indeed seems to be one of the purposes which we are appointed to fulfil in the great drama of nations; and we believe the time is at hand when we are to see a new and farther development of it. Hitherto, the "sons of the stranger" have come to us chiefly from the countries of Europe, landing on the shores of the Atlantic. Only a few years more are to pass by, and our coast on the Pacific will be alive with emigrants from the over-peopled regions of China and Japan, led to seek a new home where they can find more room and a bettered condition. But whether these crowds come from the East or from the West, we do not share in the melancholy forebodings which some feel as to the result. The union of such masses into one people congregated from various countries, always produces an improved type of man; while nations that "dwell alone and apart" fall back into imbecility and insignificance. An early vigor was given to Greece by the fusion of the Phœnicians and Egyptians with the Hellenistic tribes; and it was the mixture of the Saxons and Danes with the ancient Britons, followed by the commingling of the Normans with them all, that has led to English preponderance in arts and in arms for so long a period, and through so many regions of the globe. In this way conquest, notwithstanding its barbarities, has sometimes been overruled for the good of even the vanquished themselves.

But in this favored land, the commingling of races and its happy results are not purchased at so bloody a price. The invaders, if such they are to be called, come not as enemies, but as friends; not to demand possession of the country from its inhabitants, but to ask the privilege of uniting their wisdom and strength with ours, to give increased value to "much land which yet remains to be possessed." Nor should it be forgotten in this connection, that the strangers now coming in fresh crowds to dwell within our gates, are not so often the refuse or the surplus, as the bone and sinew of the countries from which the rod of oppression has driven them to seek a home where they can dwell in the enjoyment of freedom and plenty. In all this we see only a continuance of what has been the character and history of our nation from its beginning. There is much poetic beauty combined with important truth in the observation made by one of the most distinguished among our early divines, that "God sifted three nations for seed to sow the virgin soil of America;" and we need but to look at the leading characteristics of our various ancestors to perceive how happily they combine to form a people distinguished for power and greatness. It was the enduring strength and activity of the Anglo-Saxon, united to the staid caution and gravity of the Hollander, qualified by the elastic spirit of the French Huguenot, forming one people, and holding in the main to one religious faith, that first peopled our land and spread over it the blessings of Christianity and civilization. If they found it new and ready for any impression they might give it, they engraved on its face, features that no lapse of time can obliterate. They came to it, to erect a new empire, and to present to the world, government both civil and religious, in new aspects. They undertook a great work, and they laid the foundations deep. They had faith to do what God commanded, to go where his finger pointed; and He sent his "pillar of fire by night, and of cloud by day," to lead and to shelter them. Under difficulties and dangers which surrounded them, and from which many would have shrunk, he trained them for achievements which but few can ever equal. "A waste howling wilderness" lay before them; but "with the axe in their hand, the Bible in their pocket, and the encyclopedia at their side," they began their labors, and the wilderness became changed into a fruitful field. And surveying the land to which he brought them, in the vast length and breadth into which it has now spread, how aptly does it seem described in the language of Moses, already quoted concerning the country of the Hebrews:—"It is a good land and a large, a land of brooks of water, of fountains and depths that spring out of valleys and hills, a land of wheat and barley, of vines and honey:—a land whose stones are iron, and out of whose hills thou mayest dig brass."

Except as to the larger scale on which everything with us is laid out, there is a very striking parallel between the land of Israel as here described, and our own. What advantages had they which we have not; whether contributing to their happiness and safety at home, or facilitating their influence for good among nations abroad?

We have seen the abundance and variety in which their land yielded its produce to the labors of industry, and which distinguished it as "the glory of all lands," in its day. Our own country is so new that we have as yet examined only its surface. We can scarce be said to have commenced the experiments for testing the fecundity of the soil, or for exploring and ascertaining the stores of mineral wealth that lie hidden in its mines. And yet even at this day when its resources are so imperfectly developed, compare it with England, France, Spain, or any one country of modern times, and we must see how greatly it surpasses them in the variety and extent of its productions. Stretching through climes of every temperature, it produces every grain, plant, or fruit that can be desired for the sustenance of man, or the healthful gratification of his appetite. It yields every material for clothing that can minister to comfort or ornament, it has stored within its bowels every mineral which most effectually ministers to the strength and safety of a people; and then we have to add, that all these rich and various stores are gained only by the labor which renders them twice a blessing. With us it is " the hand of the diligent that maketh rich : " and nothing else, nothing less can do it.

We showed also, how the face of their country and its associations, furnished excitement and cultivation to the intellectual faculties of the Hebrews. With us also, mind in all its varieties has new scope and ample nutriment. Thought, and communication of thought, are free as the air. Intellect is rendered alert and bounding by the vast and inviting fields that are yet to be explored and improved ; while the taste and fancy of our artists and poets and orators are heightened by the grandeur and beauty which are spread over the face of the country, in its lofty mountains, its majestic rivers, its wide plains and seas. The materials and the excitement of thought are furnished by the scenery that environs us throughout our borders.

As to security against invasion from foreign foes ; it was scarcely more true that " Israel dwelt in safety and alone, and was not numbered among the nations," than it is true of us as a people. The wide ocean rolls between us and the kingdoms which have long proved restless and dangerous neighbors to each other ; nor is there a moral possibility of a nation growing up at our side, with strength to endanger our peace and our safety. On the contrary, every few years sees our territory widened and making fresh accessions to the strength of the nation; nor is this done by conquest, subjecting our neighbors to a colonial dependance, which they would improve the first opportunity to throw off. They come to us of their own will. They knock at our doors for adoption, as members of the national household, promising allegiance to our authority, while they ask for protection from our power.*

But there is still another point of the parallel worthy of distinct notice. It lies in the local advantages possessed by this country for easy and speedy access to all the most important nations of the earth. In this respect, we sustain, in a remarkable degree, the same relation to the world at large, in which, as we have seen, the Hebrews stood to the Eastern Hemisphere. Look at the extent of ocean which washes our shores from North to South, furnishing us with the readiest communication with every nation of our own continent. Look also at the broad Atlantic, which carries us to the door of every great nation in Western Europe. But still more, look in a different direction, and to what, until lately, has been less observed. Turn your eyes towards the vast and populous Empires of China and India, which have hitherto been reached both by Europeans and ourselves, after long and circuitous voyages, over

* Note K.

seas and around capes, that have been strewed with wrecks, till they have been made frightful Golgothas, for the mariners and merchandise of all civilized nations. The highway of commerce to those rich countries of the East, will not much longer be around the southern point of Africa, or under the burning Equator. A wiser and a safer way is fast revealing itself to the sagacious observer of events and developments in the present generation. Steam has now shown that it can be rendered quite as effective for the navigation of oceans as of rivers; and the wide Pacific, rolling between our western shores and the nations of Eastern Asia, seems formed by the Creator for the ocean steamer. Its numberless islands, that give life and variety to its bosom, are just the opportune resting places or depots to furnish what the vessel needs as she wings her way across its broad expanse of waters; and we have only to cast our eyes over the surface of our whole globe and observe the points of distance which separate both Europe and America from Eastern Asia, in order to see how inevitably our country, with its cities on the Atlantic and Pacific coasts, must soon become the great thoroughfare of wealth and knowledge travelled by the civilized world. I speak of a change which neither war, nor violence, nor cunning diplomacy, can be required to accomplish; but which will be accomplished all the sooner and better if these unholy agencies will let it alone. I speak of what is the manifest purpose of Him who hath fixed bounds to the sea and the dry land; and hath determined the courses of rivers and of mountains. I speak of what is the natural course of events, and which flow as a consequence from the works of His hand, which neither the folly nor selfishness of man can resist or defeat. But when our land shall thus have become a central point to the whole world, on the one side reaching China and the adjacent Archipelago, through the Pacific, studded with its coral isles; and, on the other, reaching the most powerful nations of Europe, through the long travelled Atlantic; who does not foresee the impulse which will then be given to the spread of our religion, our laws and institutions, and the influence which they must thenceforward have on the destinies of the whole habitable globe.

Allow me to notice one other point in this parallel. We have shown you how opportunely the establishment of the Hebrew commonwealth was adapted to prevent the utter ruin of the guilty nations whose iniquity was then full. Equally opportune was the settlement of this land and the rise of our republic. When America first came to the knowledge of Europe, so galling was the yoke of civil and ecclesiastical tyranny, and such was the determined spirit of resistance against it, that had there not been in this country a place of escape for the wronged and oppressed, an explosion would have been produced, causing blood to flow in torrents. Judge of it as the kings and princes of Europe may, this western world is the safety-valve to which they owe their preservation from an earlier and utter ruin. Had it not been provided in due season, their thrones would have been hurled to the dust by a spirit too fierce and excited to discern where justice should end and mercy should begin, and which, in its hot haste, might have confounded right with wrong, and truth with error. Cromwell was on the point of leaving England and embarking for America, when he was compelled to remain by an arbitrary order of Council, and the consequence to royalty is well known. In this new world his daring and manly spirit would have had ample scope for the accomplishment of good, without the irritation from insufferable wrongs which drove him to deeds that every one must condemn and deplore. Many a noble patriot in our land would have been a Cromwell, if not something worse, had he been compelled to act his part under Cromwell's temptations. Chafed, as the minds of men had become in the Old World, by long continued cruelty and injustice, they required the calm retirement of the New, and its great distance from the scene of their sufferings, to enable them to judge wisely and deliberately as to what were the true remedies for the evils which they could no longer endure. And now that their work is done, and institutions created by the wise and deliberate counsels of the founders of our Republic, which are alike the happiness and safety of our country; the older nations of the earth are deriving no small benefit from the freedom which we claim as our inheritance. The remark is just and true, that Old England would not have become what she is in the freedom of her subjects, if New England had never sprung from her loins. Her rulers have seen that nothing could save them from a revolution but a spirit of wise and timely concession to the rightful demands of the people; and at this day we see her "conservatives" occupying and defending ground where her advocates of "reform," not many years since, scarce ventured to take up their position. In fact, there is not a nation in Europe that has not felt, and does not now feel, our influence in curbing and restraining tyranny, or in keeping alive an ambition for freedom in the minds of the people.

I have but one concluding topic to urge. It relates to the high and responsible post which God has assigned to this country, in the great work of evangelizing and civilizing the world. No nation in Protestant Christendom stands so directly face to face with Pagan nations as ourselves. From our shores on the Pacific, we look immediately, not only on the inhospitable wilds of Siberia, but upon the vast and populous empire of China; upon Farther India, and upon the islands of Japan and the Eastern Archipelago; regions "where Satan's seat is," and where his unclean and cruel dominion, as yet, has been scarcely invaded. A new way of access to them is now opened. We have shown you how the ocean, which divides us from them, is soon to be bridged by our flying steamers freighted with the wealth of the world. While our merchants will be actively employed in gathering golden harvests from commerce with these dark and long inaccessible countries, Christians among us should be equally engaged in sending them "greater riches than the treasures of Egypt." They present a field for Gospel conquests that seems to have been reserved for the American Churches; and we should consider it a duty specially required of us to "go up and possess the land," covering it with the blessings of Christian truth and Christian freedom. No nation lies under so heavy a responsibility in this thing as the United States of America.

But we have a work to do at home as well as abroad for Christianizing the world, which, in a great degree, is peculiar to ourselves. I have alluded to the prevalence of the sentiment, that our country is the home of the emigrant, and that to furnish an asylum for the oppressed and destitute of other lands, is one of the destinies which we are appointed to fulfil. I have said, I do not share in the fears which some entertain on this subject. I do not believe that our institutions are jeopardized by the crowds seen flying to us from abroad. I entertain the higher hopes of our country when I see it becoming a Bethesda, a house of mercy for the suffering; for it thus secures to itself the blessings of them that were ready to perish. The nation has possessed a character from the beginning too distinct and enduring, too strong and determined, to be changed by any exotic influence acting upon it at this day of its maturing strength. Let wise legislation and active Christian benevolence take care that foreigners be made to understand and appreciate our civil and religious privileges; and, so far from having anything to fear, we have much to hope both for ourselves and for them by their residence in the midst of us. It is indeed true that they bring with them lamentable displays of ignorance and superstition. But we should look upon them as sent to us to be enlightened and relieved. We should consider it as so much work brought to our doors, that it may be done the more effectually. They are sent to us that they may gain lessons of wisdom, which they could not have learned so well, nor would we so earnestly have taught them, had they remained in their former homes. When they become inhabitants of a country held in common by them and ourselves, we feel that we are so shut up to our duty that the penalty of our neglect must be our own ruin; that we must give the truth to them, or lose it ourselves; and thus are we stimulated in our duty by the conviction that, while we are acting for the good of others, we are also laboring for our own welfare, and the welfare of our children in future generations.

But the good which may thus be done among "the strangers within our gates" is far from being confined to those who may live and die among us. Through them we are sowing a seed which is yet to spring up and bear its most abundant fruit in the countries from which they have come. There is an incident in New Testament history which has a pregnant meaning on this subject. When Jerusalem, on the day of Pentecost, was made the radiating point of "saving light" to the world, "there were dwellers in the city out of every nation under heaven; Parthians, and Medes, and Elamites, and the dwellers in Mesopotamia, and in Judea, and Cappadocia, in Pontus, and Asia, Phrygia, and Pamphylia, in Egypt, and in the parts of Libia about Cyrene, strangers of Rome, Jews and proselytes, Cretes and Arabians," who received the Gospel, and "were baptized in the name of Christ." The time had come when "repentance and remission of sins should be preached in his name among all nations, beginning at Jerusalem;" and here do we see the all-wise God preparing the right means for accomplishing that great end. He shed down his spirit, and brought into his church, men "of every nation under heaven," while they were "dwellers" or "sojourners" among his people, that they might be constrained and the better qualified to carry his Gospel into all the various lands from which they had come, and to which they belonged. The result was soon made known in the speed and the power with which his kingdom was spread in that day of its glory.

We believe that by a similar instrumentality the Gospel is again to be carried to distant and now darkened regions of the earth; and that such a service as was then rendered by "the dwellers at Jerusalem from every nation under heaven," will again be performed by "the sons of the stranger" now clustering to our shores from all quarters of the globe. We view them as sent to us by the overruling providence of God, that they may here learn our religion, our laws and institutions, and become the means of carrying these privileges back to the home of their fathers. In this way a new leaf is to be opened up in the history of missions. Much credit as may be due to the noble-hearted men who have gone abroad from Christian lands as missionaries to the heathen, it is vain to expect that the great mass of Pagan nations can be brought to Christianity by their labors. They can but sow the seed; "and herein is that saying true, one soweth and another reapeth." The harvest must be gathered in by those who belong to the land where the seed has taken root. No people can be so advantageously and universally instructed as where the teachers and the taught speak the same vernacular language, and sympathise with each other through the countless cords of the heart, which a foreigner cannot so happily touch. Native instructors must do the work, and they can never be so amply qualified for their task as by having lived in the midst of a people, and mingled with a people, where they have not only learned the truths of Christianity, but have also seen its practical workings, and have been witnesses of the blessings it bestows.

Our age and our country have already furnished a remarkable demonstration of this. Time has fully shown how little can be done for Africa unless by those who properly belong to her own race of the human family. Long, painfully long, has she remained what she has often been called, "*opprobrium humani generis*," the reproach of mankind, because of her deep and unrelieved degradation. Notwithstanding the most persevering efforts made by some of her best and most devoted friends, sad experience has shown that she never can be elevated and enlightened by the labors of white men. They are under the ban of her climate; and she has written her stern decree for their exclusion all along her coast, in the graves of those to whom it was allowed only to die for the cause for which they had hoped to live and labor. All now admit that if ever Africa is redeemed from darkness it must be the work of her own sons, and of their descendants, trained for a successful entrance on the service by having enjoyed the privileges of a Christian land. And since the work has passed into their hands a success has followed it that has silenced even the scoffer. "Ethiopia is stretching out her hands unto God." Regions on her coast, lately "filled with the habitations of cruelty," are blessed with the light of life. A cordon of moral health begins to surround her, not to confine pestilence within, but to exclude pirates from without, whose ruthless violence has long soaked her sands in the tears and blood of her children. Liberia is a Christian and a free country; and, like "a city set on a hill," is showing to the world what Africans can become, and can accomplish, when moulded under the power of the Gospel. It was in America, and while dwelling in the midst of us, that the men who have thus begun the work of evangelizing the land of their fathers were trained for their high enterprise; and our nation has enjoyed the opportunity of showing how successfully colonies may be planted, without entailing on them the evils of colonial dependence.

Let us also look at China. Missionary means and labors have been expended there without interruption for many years, but with comparatively small success. The land still continues walled in from the approach of the Gospel, and the inhabitants boast that its citadels of darkness remain impregnable, whether assailed by one denomination of Christians or another. Their habitual jealousy and studied contempt for foreigners seems to shut their ears against the truth which its ablest advocate may present to them; and their language is so intricate and perplexing that it costs him the labor of years before he can either speak or write it with freedom and confidence.* No argument can be required to show what an impulse would be given to the spread of Christianity in China by the native Chinaman, who, having witnessed and felt the power of the Gospel in a Christian land, would then return with a heart yearning for the salvation of his countrymen, "beseeching them, in Christ's stead, to be reconciled unto God." But where, and how are the proud jealous sons of that long secluded and wide empire to be qualified for such an important service? Not many years since it would have been scarce possible to give an answer to the question. Recent events, already noticed, suggest a reply. The advance of our nation, with her institutions both ci vil and religious, to the shores of the Pacific, was an important step in the civilization of the world; and now, when under the ægis of her protection, she is bringing to light the rich resources of that long neglected region, the dormant faculties of the various nations in Eastern Asia will soon be quickened into new activity. The Celestial Empire already begins to lose the spell which bound the Chinaman in the belief that it contains within itself every thing of value, and that every thing "on the outside" of its confines is barbarous and worthless. The new, but restless desire to learn the secret of our strength,

* Note L.

when we have opened a new way to his doors, will impel him to show himself among us. And when the Chinaman comes he will soon be followed by others. When our country shall have become, as we have described, the great highway for the commercial wealth of the world as it passes from one continent to another, it will call to our shores myriads from north, south, east and west, until every language shall be spoken, and every tribe and kindred of the human family shall be seen among us. The effect of such a state of things on the religious interests of mankind was not overlooked by the "Holy men of God, speaking as they were moved by the Holy Ghost." A commerce which will bring together countries now far distant from each other, a commerce which forms that very branch of enterprise and industry in which our nation is fast taking the lead, is distinctly described in prophetic language, as yet to have a wide-felt influence in turning the whole earth to the Lord. "Surely the isles shall wait for me, and the ships of Tarshish first, to bring thy sons from far, their silver and their gold with them, unto the name of the Lord thy God, and to the Holy One of Israel."

When I look forward to that day, a day of such large, if not measureless means of doing good to mankind, yet to be entrusted to the hands of this nation, I admit that I "rejoice with trembling." It will bring with it a responsibility to God and to man for which we should be anxious to be well prepared. Many of our sainted fathers, as Edwards, Davies, and others, "after they had served their generation, by the will of God fell on sleep" cheered to their dying hour with the conviction that from the churches in America the Gospel will be first exhibited, with that light and power which will subdue "every nation, and kindred, and tongue, and people," to the obedience of faith. Events which they could little foresee seem to be preparing the way for the fulfilment of their expectations. Are Christians amongst us animated by a zeal which corresponds with these brightening indications of God's holy providence?

FOURTH LECTURE.

In our last lecture, having alluded to the condition of the Hebrew nation while suffering their bondage in Egypt, we observed that to have given them the institutions of civil freedom, without first preparing them for it, would not have been either kindness or wisdom. The minds of the people needed to be trained to new associations, new conceptions and new standards of right, before they could be entrusted with the privileges of self-government; and we showed how this great object was promoted by their migration to another country, by their removal from Egypt to the Land of Canaan.

We have now to contemplate another step in the work of preparation, and which indeed forms a prominent feature in the constitution by which they were to be governed. I refer *to the provision made for the diffusion of knowledge throughout all classes of the people.*

It has been remarked, that "a well graduated

commonwealth is like a pyramid; the common people are its base; and in communities, as in architecture, the destruction is greatest when it begins at the foundation;" and it might have been added, that the edifice can never be strong and enduring if the foundation is not sound and well adapted to its place. Hence the indispensable importance of rendering a free people an intelligent people—of securing to them a competent education for the discharge of their relative duties to God and to man. Irrational animals may choose that which is best for their own welfare if left to themselves. They can follow their instinct, and thus best answer the purpose of their creation. To eat and to drink, to live and to die, is their beginning and their end, the sum of their destiny. "Their spirit goeth downward," says the Preacher. But, on the contrary, "the spirit of man goeth upward." He is formed for higher things. He was made to rule the world around him, and to make it the theatre of preparation for a better. He has duties to perform to his Maker and to his fellow-men, which demand inquiry, thought, and reflection; which call for divine light from above, to guide, and a right heart within, to follow where his duty and happiness require him to go. And yet see what he is when he comes into the world, where he is to act so important a part both to others and for himself. He is born, both in body and mind, a feeble creature. As his physical frame needs a mother's judicious care for its growth and development, his moral and mental faculties would remain feeble and become distorted if left to themselves; and if ever his powers are so drawn out as to render him what he is capable of becoming, he must be led to his duty, not driven to it. He is not a mere machine, nor can he be governed as such. You may, by mere force, prevent him from doing what is wrong, but you cannot, by the same means, constrain him to do what is right. You must help him to understand his duty. You must use the means which his Maker has appointed to free him from the thraldom and degradation of ignorance, and thus awaken him to a sense of the destiny before him; and then, and only then, can you expect him both to comprehend and fulfil his duties to his Maker, to himself, and also to his neighbor.

Such being the case, it is very obvious that, over and above the essential importance of instruction to men viewed as immortal beings, if they are ever to become the subjects of self-government as a nation, they must be educated for it—educated to understand and appreciate their privileges and responsibilities, and the respective duties arising out of them. Accordingly, let us see what God ordained on this point for the nation of the Hebrews when he organized them as a commonwealth.

Strange as it may perhaps seem to some of us, there has scarcely ever been a nation in which the people were so universally taught to read. That such was very generally the case in the time of our Saviour, we would infer from the manner in which he often appeals to the people, asking, "Have ye not read what Moses saith," "Have ye not read in the Scriptures," thus implying that his hearers could and did read the writings of Moses and the prophets. The same thing is plainly to be inferred when we are told respecting the inscription which Pilate placed over the head of the Redeemer at his crucifixion, "This title then read many of the Jews." But we have proof that may be viewed as still more conclusive. We may quote to you the law which impliedly enjoins it on parents, as a solemn duty, that the young should be taught to read and to study the statutes and the ordinances which God had revealed. "The words which I command thee this day," he ordains, "shall be in thy heart, and thou shalt teach them diligently to thy children." But how was this diligent instruction to be given? The command proceeds to say, "Thou shalt talk of them when thou sittest in thine house, and when thou walkest by the way, when thou liest down, and when thou risest up." But was this oral instruction all that they were bound to give? Was there no other mode of teaching enjoined? See what is added: "And thou shalt bind them for a sign upon thine hand, and they shall be as frontlets between thine eyes; and thou shalt write them upon the posts of thine house, and on thy gates." It scarcely needs to be observed that if parents were to instruct their children in God's law, by thus writing it for them; it follows that both parents and children must have been able to read it when written, for otherwise the writing would have been comparatively useless. And when you consider that in those days the art of printing had not been discovered, and that great time and labor were required in order to write the contents of the inspired volume on the posts of their doors and on their gates, you may learn the importance which the Most High attributed to the ability to read, as a means of preparing a people for the intelligent and conscientious discharge of their respective duties. Accordingly we find it to be the uniform testimony of Jewish writers that the school was to be found in every district throughout the nation, and under the care of teachers who were honored alike for their character and their station.

Nor was this all. As the divine command plainly implies, and as intelligent Jewish commentators interpret its meaning, it was not left to parents to decide whether their children should or should not be suitably educated. This duty was viewed as enjoined upon them by the authority of law; and up to this point we believe that wise legislation should come in every commonwealth. A parent should be required to educate his children if he has the ability to do it, and if not, the state should do it for him. There is nothing in such a requirement which can be accounted unjust or unreasonable. It implies no violation of a parent's rightful authority over his own family. Parental duty may be, and is enforced by the laws of the land in other cases. If a parent neglects to provide food and raiment for his children, the civil authority compels him to do it if he has the ability; and if not, it takes them out of his hands and does it in his stead. And is the body of more value than the mind; or the animal wants of a people of more consequence to public welfare than the moral and intellectual? Apart from the benefits which such laws ensure to the young themselves, in securing them against the degradation of ignorance, every well-ordered state should feel that, as it values public safety, it must not allow its youth to grow up within its own bosom in a condition of ignorance that would render them incendiaries, and pests to all its best interests.

Still farther, schools for the general education of the people were not the only institutions of learning among the Hebrews. To shed upon our earth the full and various illumination which it needs, there must be not only the lesser, but also the greater lights in the firmament; and it is from the greater that the lesser often derive their power to shine. The same laws prevail in the world of learning and of mind. The higher and greater seminaries of education are indispensable to a sound state of intellect in a people; were they to disappear, the common school would soon be shorn of its brightness. They are both parts of the same system, and they must exist and move together if the system is harmonious and complete. Accordingly there were higher institutions introduced and established among the Hebrews, under the title of "Schools of the Prophets," by which are meant seminaries where were taught, not only theology, but also other branches of knowledge which were reckoned among the pursuits of learning in that day.*

These "Schools" were under the care of men who stood high for their own intellectual attainments and their ability to impart knowledge to their

* The term "prophet" is sometimes used in Scripture not only for one who fortells future events, but also for one who is employed in giving instruction. Num. 11 : 25, 27. Also, 1 Cor. 14 : 1, 3 4.

pupils. Even Samuel, notwithstanding the abundance of his public cares, seems at times to have sought the retirement which they afforded, to refresh his mind with a review of what he had studied in earlier life, and to take a part in teaching the young scholars of the nation, who were in aftertimes to be its leading men in both Church and State. The result of such a regard for learning was what may well be called the golden age of the Hebrews, in which the nation rose to a high point of intellectual distinction. Solomon and his court were in their day the great centre of attraction for those of all nations who loved and honored knowledge. "His wisdom," we are told, "excelled all the wisdom of the children of the East country, and all the wisdom of Egypt. He spake of trees, from the cedar in Lebanon even unto the hyssop that springeth out of the wall; he spake also of beasts, and of fowl, and of creeping things, and of fishes. His songs were a thousand and five, and his proverbs three thousand." And while he excelled in the wide fields of natural science, poetry and ethics, the Temple, which still bears his name, stood before the world a monument of skill and taste, which rendered it in after ages the original model of grace, majesty, and grandeur in architecture.

Such gifted luminaries in the intellectual world

do not shine alone. They usually belong to a constellation, and the king who sets such an example is not likely to be without followers. There was indeed one cardinal feature in the Hebrew polity which was pre-eminently favorable, at all times, to the cultivation of knowledge. By divine appointment the whole tribe of Levi were set apart for the service of religion and letters; and while many were employed before the altar and in the temple, others were devoted to study; many of whom, especially in the reign of Solomon, reached a high name both for their attainments in the science of their age and the fidelity with which they made their learning available for the benefit of the people.* Thus was produced that happy conjunction in the history of knowledge, when learning

* Michaelis terms the Levites "a learned noblesse," and speaks of them as "forming a counterpoise to the democracy of the nation." Considering his views of civil government, it is perhaps not surprising that he should have been anxious to find something in the Hebrew State as an offset against its plainly democratic spirit. There was little of a "noblesse" among the Levites. While it is true, as he says, that "they were not merely a spirituality, but the literati of all the faculties," and were generally chosen to offices of importance whether in church or state; this arose from their superior knowledge and general worth of character. His idea that they were not employed in teaching the people, is utterly inadmissible. Moses declares expressly of the Levites, as such, "They shall teach Jacob thy judgments and Israel thy law." To

bestowed honor on the learned, and the learned brought honor to learning; when the highest attainments were deemed of value, not according as they gave distinction to him who had reached them, but according as they tended to improve and to bless the whole family of man. Among the Hebrews there was no monopoly of knowledge by a favored few. Intelligence was general in the degree and of the kind adapted to the various duties and pursuits of those among whom it was spread. The tongue and the pen of even learned royalty were industriously employed in giving to knowledge that condensed and practical form which might bring it within the reach, and make it available for the advantage of all, of the shepherd and vine-dresser, as well as "the Sons of the Prophets." When the learned act with this generous and dutiful spirit, they always reap according as they sow. The minds

have been "without a teaching priest" is described as the cause of the general impiety and adversity which at times overtook the nation; and the return of the Levites to their duty as teachers is more than once mentioned as among the first things enjoined by rulers and kings who arose as reformers of prevailing abuses. 2 Chron. 15 : 3. 17 : 7–9. 30 : 22. 35 : 3. Nehemiah, 8 : 7, 8. The labors of the Levites may not have been precisely like those of our parish clergymen; but whether it was in the school of higher or lower degree, or in the assembly of worship, the tribe of Levi were ordinarily considered as the appropriate instructors.

of those who receive instruction will re-act upon the minds of those who give it, imparting to them higher aspirations, and leading them to greater acquisitions. If, as geologists tell us, there are countries where the whole land is constantly rising higher and higher above the level of the sea, the mountains must rise as well as the valleys; and in every wisely adjusted system for the intellectual education of a nation, when the mass of the people are improved in intelligence, the attainments of the more learned will be advanced in a like proportion. All will rise together.

These provisions for the diffusion of knowledge which we find among the Hebrews have been sanctioned by universal history as inseparably interwoven with national prosperity. No people can rise from civil or social degradation without education; and no ruler deserves the reputation of a public benefactor who would not give his unremitting care to this object, as of paramount importance. The "good king Alfred," as he is often called, arose at a time when nothing less than a spirit like his could have saved his country from entire subversion. He expressly attributes its worst evils to the prevalence of ignorance, and he began his measures of reform by inviting distinguished scholars from abroad, by endowing literary institutions for the cultivation of learning, at the same time establishing schools throughout the land for the education of the people, requiring every parent to send his children to be taught, and giving public employment only to such as had made satisfactory proficiency in knowledge. He went farther still. He added the influence of his own example, not only as a diligent and successful student, but in preparing, with his own pen, books for the intellectual and moral improvement of all classes among his subjects. Before his death the whole face of affairs in the land was changed: and in a work, said to be still extant, he congratulates himself on the prosperity which had sprung from general education.

The mantle of Alfred is often said to have fallen upon Edward the Sixth. The wonderful mind of that prince would have rendered him another "admirable Crichton," if he had been simply a scholar and not a king. In wisdom he was as far beyond his own years as he was before the age of the world in which he lived. When he took counsel, as he tells us, how he should most effectually benefit the Commonwealth, he pronounced "good education, first in order, and first in dignity and degree," and declared his purpose to "show his device therein." Alas! death cut him off in the midst of his plans for the freedom and happiness of his people, removing him from a world in which, at that day, he seems to have been too wise and too good to find those who would co-operate with him for the welfare of his race. His death has been considered by many as the greatest calamity with which England was ever overtaken; and her philanthropists and statesmen of late have been led to feel the importance of the work he contemplated, and are making it the "question of questions" how to diffuse suitable education among the mass of the people.

The service rendered to Scotland by her parish schools is known to every one at all acquainted with her history. So deep was her degradation before she introduced them, that one of her leading patriots was led to propose the introduction of domestic servitude as a remedy for the vagrancy and low crime which had overspread the country. Since she gave her people education, she has produced a race of men known through the world for their shrewd intelligence and successful industry. If we look at the enactments of Holland for educating the children of that Republic, and which were enforced by the authority of both Church and State, we can see how she arose to the greatness that once distinguished her. To Prussia, however, belongs the credit of having recently set an example that has given a new impulse to the cause of popular education in Europe. The value of instruction depends on the qualifications of the teacner ; and with a wise regard to this important principle, Prussia created Normal Institutions for the education of teachers, and also established schools in every district of the country, to which every parent is required by law to send his children, unless he gives satisfactory proof to the competent authority that he is educating them at home at his own expense. The effect of these regulations is that every child in the Prussian dominions receives, at a suitable age, an education in such branches as are connected with the ordinary purposes of life. Within a few years also a special ordinance has been passed directing that a Bible be placed in the hands of every teacher in the public schools, as an official acknowledgment of the truth of Christianity. The consequences which must flow from such a system of instruction can be easily foreseen. Neither civil nor religious abuses can long endure when the mind of the public becomes so effectually enlightened respecting the rights and duties of rulers and ruled. We hazard little in the prediction that Prussia will take the lead among the nations of Europe in many of the reforms which are approaching.

But to the ancestors of our own country we may turn for the best of proofs, showing the importance of general education for the welfare of the people.

They were Bible men. In whatever they did for themselves or for others, for private or for public welfare, they acted on Bible principles. And whether they were Hollanders, or Huguenots, or Pilgrims, on this point they had but one mind, they adopted but one rule as to the rising generation. It was, that every child must be taught, at the charge of its parents if they were able ; at the charge of the public if they were not. And from that, as the root, has sprung the tree of our national prosperity, which is spreading forth its branches so luxuriantly. If its growth is not to be checked, and its beauty marred, we, in our day, and our children after us, must carry out this principle, which they esteemed so fundamental in both their civil and religious systems. It furnishes no small gratification to both the patriot and the Christian to see constant proofs that their zeal for the blessings of education is fully alive in the nation. Widely and rapidly as we are carrying our free institutions into the wilderness, every new Territory and State makes it a leading point in her policy to set apart lands or other resources for schools; and in the older States "the school fund" is guarded with a jealously that shows how universally public sentiment sympathises with the education of the people. Every party in politics, and every sect in religion, unite in the belief that general ignorance would be certain ruin; and that if we expect it "to be well with us and with our children after us," the civil anthorities should make it a matter of imperative obligation that a child should be educated, as much as that a child should be fed and clothed. The curse of ignorance is worse than the curse of nakedness and hunger. It is often the cause of both, and of still more ruinous effects. "It is only," says a great statesman, "it is only when every child can read its Bible, that every family will have its meal." He told but a part of the story. When every child can read its Bible, every family will have something more than its meal. Mere animal comforts will not be all that a people thus educated will crave and will have. They will have their meal, and with it the civil and religious institutions which ensure elevation of mind and of morals, and form the true glory and strength of any nation.

These observations at once introduce a view of the subject to which I wish to call especial attention. I mean the duty and expediency of maintaining the use of the Bible in our schools. Did my limits permit I would respectfully suggest the inquiry to professors and lecturers in our higher seminaries of learning, whether the Bible receives due attention as a book abounding with classical beauties, when they are instructing their students in belles lettres studies. A heathen critic has referred to the words, "Let there be light, and there was light," as the most perfect specimen of the sublime which he could quote from any writing extant in his day. It were to be wished that a greater number of our instructors in criticism would follow his example, and draw out more fully into view the striking illustrations of grandeur and sublimity, grace and beauty, dignity and simplicity, whether in history or poetry, which are to be found in the Holy Scriptures. Had Blair and Kaimes, and others quoted, we will not say less frequently from Demosthenes and Homer, from Cicero and Virgil, from Addison and Shakspere, but more frequently from Moses, David, Isaiah and Paul, their illustrations might have been more perfect and convincing; and while the mind of the pupil was taught to admire the casket, his heart might have been led to realize the value of the diamond it contains.

But my chief object at present is to assert the importance of maintaining the use of the Bible in our common schools as a book for the scholar who is learning the elementary branches of education. It has always been surprising to me that in a Christian land any question should ever have been raised on the subject. The answer is so obviously dictated by common sense, that, to a mind devoid of prejudice, there seems no room for doubt. The great object of education is to form the taste, to elicit the powers and habitudes of thought, and to give purity and rectitude to the heart and life. If there is any one book which has been proved by the history of all time to be the best book for accomplishing these invaluable ends, that is *the* book with which every learner should be made familiar. Let him learn from others in their respective places and according to their respective claims; but let none of them displace this from its priority. Let it stand upon its merits, and according to its merits tried and proved by its fruits through countless generations, let it be regarded. This is the plain and common sense answer to the question, so tortured and vexed in our day, of whether the Bible should be read in our schools. If we can be furnished with any other book that promises more effectually to improve the mind or the heart, and which makes its lessons so plain and simple that a child can understand and feel them, then we have not a word to say. But if, for these invaluable purposes, and in these rare attributes, the Bible stands peerless and alone, then have we every thing to say in proof that learners should take their lessons from its inspired pages.

What then are the facts, and what the judgment of the wise and the good respecting the best book for a learner? Would they give us the Bible, or have they discovered something better? When the subject came before the mind of that accomplished scholar and jurist, Sir William Jones, he declared that "The Scriptures contain, independently of their divine original, more true sublimity, more exquisite beauty, more important history, pure morality, and finer strains both of poetry and eloquence than could be collected within the same compass from all other books that were ever composed in any age or in any idiom." And we should add that, while his judgment is confirmed by the testimony of the learned in all professions, it is in fullest accordance with the views of the best masters who have devoted themselves to the business of education.

But there is something still further to be said of the Bible as a book for learners in a country like ours. Here the English language is the language of the nation; and not only is it fast rooting out every other which has hitherto prevailed in different parts of the land, but it is yet to be the great language of communication throughout the civilized world. On these accounts it should be made a leading subject of study in our schools. But although the essential beauties of the Bible, which are so forcibly and comprehensively described in the words we have just quoted, cannot be lost in any language or dialect into which it is faithfully rendered; yet into no language has the rich meaning of the inspired volume been so fully and happily conveyed as our own; and in no book which can be put into the hands of a reader is there such a "well of English undefiled" as in our English Bible. Both these points are now matters of general consent. In the words of Adam Clarke, "our translators have not only made a standard translation, but they have made their translation the standard of the language. The English tongue in their day was not equal to such a work; but God enabled them to stand as upon Mount Sinai, and *crane* up their country's language to the dignity of the originals, so that after the lapse of two hundred years the English Bible is, with very few exceptions, the standard of purity and excellence of the English tongue."

The classical and accomplished Dr. Beattie describes it as "a striking beauty in our English Bibles that, though the language is always elegant and nervous, and for the most part very harmonious, the words are all plain and common, without affectation of learned terms."

"In no book," said the eloquent Fisher Ames, "is there so good English, so pure and elegant; and by teaching all the same book, they will speak alike, and the Bible will justly remain the standard of language as well of faith."

"Indeed," says another high authority,* "when we reflect that the Bible has been regarded as a model of correct expression by the ablest critics, that it has been more read than any other English book, that the nature of its subjects and the character of the people have given it, more than any other book, a hold upon the imagination and the feelings, we do not wonder at the extent to which its language has become the basis both of prose and of verse, and even, to some extent, of common conversation. The Bible is not subject to the fluctuations of taste."

It surely will not be said that there is any other book which even approaches the Bible in such testimony on its behalf, showing its value to enrich and discipline the mind, by furnishing it with both the best materials and the best models for thought.

But education has done only a part of its work when it enlightens the mind and refines the taste of the scholar. The affections and conduct must

* Biblical Repository and Theological Review: p. 185, vol. 8. The quotation is from an interesting and valuable article, entitled "The English Bible," and which contains several other testimonies of a like import with those we have recited. The whole article is replete with important facts and statements, presented with much clearness and force.

be reached as well as the understanding; and when I ask for the best book to improve the heart and the life of the learner—what shall it be? Can any one say that, in the whole range of writings, ancient or modern, there is a book to compare with the Bible for this great purpose? Go among the old and young who exhibit a pure life, a right heart, and a "conscience void of offence towards God and towards man," and to what will they ascribe the influence that has opened their eyes to see their duty and inclined their hearts to pursue it? They will all refer you to the Bible and the sacred truths it contains. Then look at the opposite picture: Go among them who are the foes of heaven, and the plague of earth, who have become so hardened in the long practice of deep iniquity that "their neck is a sinew of iron, and their brow brass," and ask them what they know of the Bible. You find them strangers to the very name. It has been to them in youth and in years a book unknown, and hence the hardened and hopeless obduracy of their case. Or let us turn again to a still different class of transgressors, to those who may have wandered far from the paths of duty, but who in their early days have been taught to read the Bible. Far as they may have gone in evil, you always find in their bosoms a chord that can be touched, a tender point in the conscience which remains as a token that there is hope in their case, and that, like the prodigal of old, they may one day come to themselves. Let the mind in early life be Bible trained, let it be brought into frequent and familiar contact with these inspired pages, and a seed is sown that cannot die while the man lives; it may be hidden by a long winter, but a season of spring usually follows, when the bud and the blossom will put themselves forth. Now where is the book that in these respects can dispute the palm with the Bible? What its name, and who its author? By what tests has it been tried, and what testimony can it bring to vouch for its claims?

"Bring me the book," said the far-famed Sir Walter Scott, when he felt that his last days were approaching. And when he was asked, "What book shall we bring?" he replied, "Oh! why ask me what book. There is but one book; but one book in the world that deserves the name, it is the Bible." This was the testimony of a man who had perused countless volumes, and in all the most attractive departments of human knowledge; the productions of whose own pen had fascinated myriads of old and young through the civilized world. And yet his last and truthful testimony to the value of all that had been written, or could be read, was in the memorable words, "There is but one book; but one book in the world that deserves the name, it is the Bible."

There is still another view of the subject. It relates to schools which share in the bounty of the State. This public provision for the education of the people, we have seen, is more or less interwoven with the policy of several of the most enlightened countries of Europe, and especially with that of our own. On what principle is the measure to be justified? What makes it either the right or the duty of government to employ the resources of a nation for the purposes of education? The thing is both justified and required, on the principle that the State is bound to promote and secure the best means for giving strength and stability to her own institutions, for the prevention as well as the punishment of crime, and for advancing the general welfare of the public. It is simply because education is essential to these great ends of government, that a State, as such, can either claim the right, or make it her duty to employ the public property for the purposes of general instruction, or of diffusing the elements of knowledge. Ignorance is the parent of crime and degradation, and the State has the right to educate if she has the right to punish, inasmuch as she is equally bound to use all due means for the prevention of crime, and to punish it when it has been committed.

This being a position which few accomplished statesmen would now think of either questioning or denying, the important inquiry arises, what must education be, and what must it include, if it is to be made subservient to public welfare, so as to justify the State in bestowing it or in giving her aid to acquire it? It is not to be denied that there is a kind of education which may render men more dangerous enemies to the Commonwealth than if they had remained in ignorance. To elicit and strengthen the understanding, without educating the conscience and the affections, only increases the powers of the man to do evil, without putting them under the control of those faculties which were designed to regulate and direct them for the accomplishment of good. You educate but a part of the man, and accordingly as you raise him from the level of a brute, you convert him into the shape of a fiend. The more power you give him, the more mischief is he likely to produce. You act as if putting weapons of death into the hands of a madman. It is plain that in educating men after this manner the State should have neither part nor lot. She should be careful to have no share in schooling men for guilt, or transgression of her own laws. There are schools, however, which lead directly to these results. And where do we meet with them? The statistics of crime present us with an array of facts on this point that neither infidelity nor sophistry can overlook or invalidate. It is found that crime, especially crime against society or social institutions, spreads among a people according as education becomes general, if unaccompanied by the moral influences which the Bible is the great means of producing on the minds of old and young who are familiar with its inspired pages.* It then necessarily follows that if the State bestows of her bounty for the purposes of education, she abandons the only principle which can justify the measure, she defeats her own ends unless she connects moral with intellectual training. Her schools may otherwise become nurseries of criminals.

Besides, as a corrupt people can never remain long a free people, this moral culture is not more indispensable for the prevention of crime than for the preservation of national liberty. There is nothing in that venerated record of human wisdom, "the farewell address of Washington," which is more valuable or memorable than his sentiments on this very subject. "It is substantially true," he says, "that virtue or morality is a necessary spring of popular government. The rule indeed extends with more or less force to every species of free govern-

* Note M.

ment." And that he might leave no doubt respecting the source of that morality which is so essential to freedom, he uses the explicit language, "Let us with caution indulge the supposition that morality can be maintained without religion. Whatever may be conceded to the influence of refined education on minds of peculiar structure, reason and experience both forbid us to expect that national morality can prevail in exclusion of religious principles." Indeed, there is neither hazard nor rashness in the declaration that civil freedom in its true meaning, and as we enjoy it, never existed in a nation where the religion which Washington acknowledged, the religion of the Bible, did not exist along with it; or where the Bible itself was not read and believed by the people. We may challenge contradiction of this assertion. Let us be told, if it can be done, of a single land in which you find a really free people without the Bible in the hands of the people. We have seen that the freedom of Pagan Greece and Rome was rather tyranny in a modified form, than the liberty and security combined, which equally maintains the rights of rich and poor, strong and weak. Abuses were tolerated and applauded by some of their wisest men, which in our nation would lead to revolution. Their academies and schools, notwithstanding the taste and talent which they combined for the purposes of instruction, availed but little to create in the public mind the sound views and right feelings, without which civil freedom is rather a shadow than a reality. Modern times, too, are giving us frequent examples to teach the same salutary lesson, and which, we may observe, the world seems slow to learn. Half a century since, France made her first effort to become a free nation, and with all in her favor that could be derived from "the influence of refined education." She began by burning the Bible. The result was soon seen. She escaped from chains which wore the rust of ages, only to be fettered by others that were steeped in her own blood. And I must here add, that in the fierce and agonizing throes of nations in Europe, now struggling for freedom, I scarce dare hope for a much better issue. I fear that with some of them the Most High has a Bible controversy to plead; a controversy which will be seen to have a most portentous meaning, and in which he will vindicate the outraged honor of his own Word, by writing the sin of the offending nations in their punishment. They have shed the blood of martyrs, of martyrs "who were slain for the Word of God, and for the testimony which they held." They put to death those "servants of the Most High," avowedly because of their love to God's Word, their unyielding purpose to possess it, to read it, and be governed by it. In some of these nations who thus made war upon the truth, the arm of the persecutor prevailed till the light of the Bible was extinguished in the blood of those who loved it too dearly to part with it but with their lives. With its expiring light the last glimmerings of civil freedom expired also. And now, when these same nations, roused by a sense of continued oppression and wrong, are struggling after what they can neither get nor keep without the enlightening influence of the Bible on the minds of the people, in righteous retribution, they may be left to "weary themselves with the multitude of their councils," until, having been made to feel that they are "laboring in the fire," they will turn and put merited, though long withheld honor, on that holy Volume, which was given both for the salvation of man and "for the healing of the nations." Let them restore the Bible where it was, and send it where perhaps it never yet has been, throughout all their borders, and then we may hope to see them contending for a freedom that deserves the name, and their contest crowned with victory.

There is still another consideration in this connection which shows the deep interest of the State in the moral culture of her people. Wherever an enlightened and Bible Christianity has become the predominating sentiment of the public mind, it renders a nation invincible in the defence of their civil rights. It makes courage and fortitude not only matters of ambition, but matters of conscience. It creates among all classes of the people a singleness of object, a unity and sympathy of feeling that nothing but Christianity is adequate to produce; and when the mass of a nation are governed by such high motives they have a power for self defence that defies every invader. When Spain made war upon the freedom of the United Netherlands, her gigantic strength had, in one sense, spread itself over both hemispheres. She was animated by every motive of pride and revenge that could render her strong and determined in the conflict; but still she was baffled and defeated after a long and bloody war in which she poured forth her blood and treasure like water; and the States of Holland showed to the world that where a people, however inconsiderable as to numbers, love their freedom, and are animated by Christian principle in defence of it, they are not to be subdued.*

* It may be thought that the late overthrow of Hungary is an exception. Quite the reverse. If Hungary had been like Holland, in the unanimity of her people, and in the diffusion of Christian intelligence and Christian principle, her liberty would not have been lost by the treachery or weakness of any one man, nor could even Russia and Austria combined have subdued her.

The same conclusion may be drawn from the history of our own country. When she arose to assert her freedom, her population amounted to barely three millions, her resources for war were limited and scanty, and yet she entered upon a conflict with an empire whose combined military and naval power had then no equal among the nations of the earth; and undismayed by the reverses which at times met her arms during a struggle of seven years, she came out of the contest with her rights maintained and her independence achieved. The Bible, which her statesmen and warriors had been taught to read in her schools, they carried with them into the camp and the councils of the Republic; and the high moral sentiment which they had derived from this fountain of wisdom carried them triumphantly through every peril and suffering.

Let it not be said in reply that under a government like ours, which views with equal favor all denominations of Christians, there are insuperable objections against the introduction of religious culture into schools that are patronized by the State. There is no real difficulty in the case if properly presented. In view of every great measure, involving moral duty, there are always men who "see a lion in the way," and with whom the wish is father to the thought. The lion is in the way of those whose imaginations are predisposed to conjure up some formidable obstacle as an apology for not going forward. There would be difficulty in the case before us, if the Bible could not be viewed as a separate book from the distinguishing creeds and confessions of faith which different denominations draw from it, while, at the same time, they all unite in regarding it as the only and infallible record of divine truth. However valuable may be these creeds or articles of belief, pre pared by the hands of men as bonds of union for those who embrace them; we do not admit that in our schools, enjoying endowment from the State, religion should be taught in any or all of those dis tinctive forms. But the Bible is the common property and common treasure of all who take the ground of common Christianity; and we insist that a high place be given to this book in training the young, which corresponds with the precedence which all agree in assigning to it as the supreme and unerring rule of faith and of practice, as the great and primary fountain of that wisdom and righteousness which are equally essential to the welfare of a nation and the happiness of man. It is one of the peculiar attributes of the Bible that it can speak to the heart and conscience, moulding them after its own image, with a power that no other book either contains within itself or can exercise on the minds of its readers. And when we require that a place may be assigned to it in our schools as a book for learners, which shall belong to no others, we simply require that it may be placed where it can have occasion and opportunity for displaying this proof of its own divinity, and for so influencing the minds of its readers while "young and tender," "that our sons may be as plants grown up in their youth, that our daughters may be as corner stones polished after the similitude of a palace."

And when I ask for this public acknowledgment of the great charter of Christianity, I ask for nothing more than is already incorporated in our laws as a nation. Christianity, essential Christianity, not, be it remembered, as any one sect may embrace it, but essential Christianity as contained in the Bible, is part and parcel of the common law of the land.* We see this in every Sabbath observed as a day of rest by our legislatures and by our civil authorities. To what precept or command do our makers of law and ministers of law yield obedience, in thus observing one day out of seven, if it is not the command of God speaking in his Bible? We see it in the time-honored practice of opening our halls of legislation with the solemnities of daily worship. We see it in every day of public thanksgiving or humi-

* Note N.

liation appointed or recommended by our rulers. In these and other instances which we might quote, the State acknowledges the Bible, or the religion of the Bible, as interwoven with our social institutions. Such too is the dictate of enlightened public opinion, a power stronger than either the legislature or the magistrate, and to which both are always constrained to bow. It ever has been, and we trust ever will be, the wise decision of a vast majority in our nation, to recognise and acknowledge Christianity in every due form, and on every proper occasion; and the man who finds himself aggrieved by it must not complain that he is deprived of his rightful liberty. He has all the liberty which a man in a minority can reasonably claim. He has the liberty not to undo and unsettle every thing done and approved by the majority of those around him, but the liberty to go where he can find institutions and neighbors more to his mind. He has "the world before him where to choose," but we must fear that he has not "Providence his guide."

We have not forgotten the trite objection, that the Bible is a sectarian book, which, as a matter of conscience, some men cannot allow their children to read. This is the mere cant of infidelity. The Bible a sectarian book! As well might it be said that the Most High is a sectarian God. The Bible is an emanation from himself. It has neither spirit nor attribute which he does not acknowledge as belonging to himself. And to talk of those who cannot allow their children to read the Bible without a violation of conscience, is the same thing as to say it violates the conscience of a parent to have his child made acquainted with the God that made him. The very worst of crimes have often sought shelter under the perverted name of conscience. It has been plead for burning martyrs at the stake, and for setting at naught every thing sacred in faith, justice, and mercy. If nothing is ever to be required or enjoined by public authority, against which any man may see fit to plead his conscience, the world may as well stand still at once. Human society cannot advance a single step. It cannot keep the ground it has gained. It must fall back till every obligation of civilized life is broken. It is against the conscience of some men that one should possess any property beyond the supply of his bodily wants, while another is either hungry or unclothed. It is against the conscience of others that the marriage covenant should still be held sacred, and that the domestic relations should still be maintained and enforced. A blind conscience, which has the opportunity of becoming enlightened and informed, and yet remains in darkness, is equally guilty and inexcusable as a hard heart which has the means of being softened and purified, and yet retains its obduracy. Such is the conscience that would prevent a child from learning the will of its Maker, as revealed in the Bible. We can make no terms with it.

In conclusion, let it be remembered that the whole responsibility of educating the young does not lie on the State, however important may be her part in the duty. There is much to be done for this object which, in a country like ours, cannot be done in the Common School. Every parent may do much in his own family, every pastor may do much in his own church to "train up a child in the way he should go." But in addition to all this, there is a machinery now at work, and which is admirably adapted to take up the work of instruction where the Common School leaves it off. I refer to our Sunday Schools: and but to name them is to praise them. They are known by their fruits, their fruits among teachers and taught. I view them as among the first of the movements in our day for the prosperity and spread of religion in any land, but as especially adapted to the condition and wants of our own.

And here you see how beautifully our system of government works. The Bible is the only standard of divine truth known to the State, and as such she can consistently place it in all her schools; and when instruction is to be given in the distinctive doctrines by which various denominations stand divided from each other, the State leaves this work to be done by the families and churches to which the youth respectively belong. If any of them choose to support schools in which their peculiar creeds shall be taught, conjointly with the different branches of general education, the State interposes no objection. On the contrary, she guards the institution against injustice and wrong as carefully as if it were fostered and sustained by her own bounty. She simply declares that she confines her direct aid to instruction in what the great mass of her people unite in receiving as both according to truth and conducive to the public welfare. And in this holy duty of training the young in our land, let the State fulfil her duty with a liberal hand; let parents and churches be faithful in their respective spheres, and how bright the prospect which opens before us! With the mind of the nation unfettered, and buoyant as our free institutions make it; with the Bible in the hand of every youth as soon as he is able to read it; and a sanctuary of worship and instruction open to every inquirer, whether old or young, who has the will to enter it; there is a healing and an enlightening influence abroad among the mass of the people that in the end will dispel every delusion, though, for a time, it may mislead and deceive. Truth is thus left to do her own work with her own weapons; and with us, as with every nation, it will yet be found that, "Truth is great, and will prevail."

FIFTH LECTURE.

In our last two Lectures we have dwelt on the principal means by which God prepared the Hebrew nation for the privileges and responsibilities of civil freedom. He removed them, as we showed you, to a new country eminently adapted to the purposes which he intended to fulfil, both towards them, and through them, towards the nations of the earth. He also distinguished them from every other people by a wide diffusion of intelligence through all classes, enabling them to understand and discharge their duties as men, and members of the Commonwealth.

But while he thus made provision for cultivating the mind of the nation, he did not overlook their physical condition. Such a competency as will secure a people against hunger and nakedness, is quite as important in its place as the spread of intelligence, in order to render them contented and happy; nor can free civil institutions exist any length of time in a nation where the mass of the people are permitted to sink into the degradation of poverty, and where wealth rolls her streams only into the hands of a few. The destruction which such a state of things would have brought on the fair fabric of freedom which

God established among the Hebrews was foreseen by his all-seeing eye; and to secure them against the evils of degrading want on the one hand, and of corrupting luxury on the other, he prescribed their pursuits and condition in life with extraordinary care.

Nomadic life is always more or less allied to barbarism, and to reclaim men from the habits of wandering hordes, and to give them a fixed dwelling place, a residence around which shall cluster the humanizing attachments of home, must always be viewed as a first step in social improvement. It is obvious that in order to effect this great end a man must have property in land—he must be enabled to look on some suitably defined portion of the earth as his own. Rousseau's favorite saying, "the first man who enclosed a field and called it mine is the author of all the social ills that followed," is not only false, but among the most glaring falsehoods which even Rousseau ever uttered. This sentiment too, which came from his pen nearly a century since, reminds us that there is nothing new under the sun. The Socialists, or Communitists, or whatever be the name by which they would be called, who, in our day, would annul all rights of individual property, and would have every thing belong to every man, and yet nothing to any man, are not entitled to claim originality in their views. They are but the followers of one whose wild notions on all subjects made it matter of doubt whether he was most of the infidel or of the madman.

To give a man the ownership of the soil on which he dwells, is the only effectual way to encourage and secure the cultivation of it; and while the wealth of a nation is thus promoted by his industry, both his possessions and his occupation tend to create that sense of independence and habit of sobriety and endurance which form the distinguishing character of a free people. Accordingly, when the Hebrews were to become the depositaries of divine truth and human rights, the Most High gave them laws which were designed to render them generally both owners and cultivators of land, and to give agriculture importance and honor in public estimation. As these ordinances involve great principles which lie at the very foundation of well organized society, let us look at them with care, and see how the observance of them among the people tended to cherish piety towards God, and both freedom and good government among themselves.

When the nation was planted in the land of promise the tribes drew their various inheritances by lot, according to a divine command. But when this was done, the law next directed that a portion of land should be allotted to every Hebrew, which was to be his for ever, which he was to cultivate during his life, and which his children after him were to take as their heritage. Except the tribe of Levi, for whom other provision was made as the ministers of religion and knowledge, every Israelite, who was the head of a family, was thus rendered a proprietor and tiller of the soil. But there was another peculiar provision. The land thus allotted to a man might pass away from his possession through his misfortune or improvidence, and his family be thus reduced to poverty, their paternal inheritance being irrecoverably lost. Such disasters we see occurring among ourselves every day. To secure the Hebrews against this degradation, and to preserve the equality which had been originally established, no landed estate could be alienated for more than fifty years. This was a leading ordinance in the polity of the Hebrews, and created a marked distinction between them and other nations; a distinction too, as we will see hereafter, which was of essential importance in promoting both public and private welfare. In Egypt, the country which they had just left, the land throughout belonged to the king; and the husbandmen, far from being proprietors of the fields on which they bestowed their labor, were rather tenants, paying a permanent rent into the royal treasury. So it long continued to be in other kingdoms of the world. And so the Hebrews were forewarned it would be with them as a consequence of their folly in choosing to be under a king. "He will take your fields," said Samuel, "and your vineyards, and your oliveyards, even the best of them, and give them to his servants. And he will take the tenth of your seed, and the tenth of your sheep, and ye shall be his servants."* Far different was the condition of the people while they were contented to live under the form of government which the Most High gave them at their settlement in the land of promise. Then every man was not only acknowledged the owner of his land for ever and unalienably, but he "sat under his vine and his fig tree, and there was none to make him afraid." The only estates which could be called entailed were those belonging to the men who would both cultivate and occupy them, thus rendering the husbandman the only hereditary nobleman of the nation. For it should be remembered, this law did not apply to the ownership of houses in cities. They might pass away from a man like his gold or silver; but his

* The manner in which Ahab sought Naboth's vineyard shows how faithfully this picture was drawn, and how recklessly the kings of Israel seized upon a landed inheritance, setting at nought the rights of their subjects and the ordinance of God.

property in land which he was to cultivate for the sustenance of himself and his family, could never be permanently alienated. Though for a few years it might cease to be his, when the year of Jubilee came round, his inheritance was by law restored to him, and he was enabled to begin the world anew. Indeed, a special law provided that any one who had parted with his land might recover it at any time, through himself or "his nearest of kin," by paying to the holder whatever might be esteemed as the reasonable profits from the property until the coming Jubilee. These ordinances secured the people against that feudal tyranny which has overrun every eastern country at one time or another, and created a degrading bondage, at war with the happiness, and too often with the innocence of the many, who were held as vassals and serfs of the few.*

Such being the fundamental laws of the State as to agriculture, it naturally followed that the occupation of the husbandman became general among the people, and was held in high honor. Their best and greatest men were more or less cultivators of the soil. Saul, when made king, was found with his oxen. Elisha, when called to be a prophet, was employed in following the plough; and

* Note O.

concerning Uzziah, one of the best kings of Judah, we are told that "he loved husbandry."

Let it be observed, there is nothing in these ordinances, or in the pursuits growing out of them, which was either designed or calculated to discourage commerce and the arts. So far as they had any bearing on these two great sources of national prosperity and high civilization, they were designed to show that both arts and commerce must be sustained by the cultivation and products of the earth; and that amidst all the branches of human industry, a priority belongs to agriculture, in its influence on the moral and physical welfare of man—a truth too often overlooked. He would show himself equally a novice in political economy and in true philanthropy, who would array any one pursuit of human life against the others. To give to the body politic the symmetry which shall render it healthful and vigorous, all the branches of human industry must be nourished and protected according to their respective claims, and these will be found to vary according to times and circumstances in the history of the world. But whether it be the merchant, the mechanic, the man of learning, or the agriculturist; every one who surveys the relations which the various pursuits of a prosperous nation have to each other, will turn to the cultivation of the earth as that which forms the basis of wealth and power to the state, and diffuses moral and physical health most widely through a whole community; and while he attributes to commerce, to the arts, and to learning their own honored places, in promoting not only agriculture itself, but also intelligence, refinement, and good will among men, he will hold that the mass of a people must have the country for their home, and the pursuits of the country for their occupation, if they would possess the leading characteristics which are so essential to civil freedom.

To inculcate these important truths was a chief design of the laws which gave to agriculture such a prominence in the Hebrew nation; and the effect of agricultural life upon their character and condition must be known to every one acquainted with their history. It produced among the people generally a bodily strength and activity, and a power of endurance that tended to render them equally formidable in war and successful in the labors of industry during times of peace. It made their whole country throughout like one continued garden, the very rocks, we are told, being covered with mould to produce vegetation, and the hills being tilled to their highest summits. The land was thus enabled to support a population that might otherwise seem incredible; and at the same time it furnished the means not only for the active exchange of commodities, which was usual at their principal festivals, but for that extensive foreign commerce which, in the days of Solomon, so enriched the nation that "gold was laid up as dust, and the gold of Ophir as the stones of the brooks." Nor was it until a spirit of cupidity, pride, and luxury, generated by the gains of commerce, had brought into neglect the labors of the husbandman, that the strong arm of the nation was palsied, and she fell a prey to her invaders.

But there were still further advantages resulting from these enactments, and which had an important moral influence on the people.

They stripped poverty of its worst evils. "The poor ye have always with you," saith our Saviour, and the words are only another version of the declaration of Moses, "the poor shall not cease out of the land." But although poverty cannot be entirely prevented while sin and sorrow abound in the world, its bitterest evils may be greatly alleviated. Its sense of degradation may be removed. Its squalidness and despair may be cured. Its bitterest sufferings may be lightened by the hope of better days either for the man himself or for his children. You may save him from becoming the malignant enemy, or the inert burden of his race. You may save him from the heart-breaking pang of looking at the home where his fathers dwelt, and he himself was born, now in the hands of a stranger, and never again to acknowledge him as its owner. Such was the effect of the law which restored to every man his landed inheritance on the year of Jubilee. It kept his heart whole. It preserved within him a love of home. It kept alive, even among the most destitute, a spirit of hope, and a love of independence; for every one could look forward to a day when the home of his fathers, and the place of his own birth, would again be in the possession of himself or of his children. His flocks and herds might have been taken from him, and have gone for ever. His best ornaments might have been given up, never to be regained. But the land on which he might dwell, and by his industry recover his lost place among his brethren, was always there, and his claim upon it indefeasible.

Allied to this was another important public advantage growing principally out of the laws and ordinances to be observed at the year of Jubilee. I *refer to their happy effect in preventing the evils of accumulated debt.* Oppressive indebtedness, whether public or private, is one of the worst calamities that can afflict a people. It often weakens the tone of sound moral feeling, and "leads into temptation" too strong to be resisted. There were several ordinances in the Hebrew Commonwealth bearing directly on this subject, and all of them framed on the principles of obvious wisdom. Experience shows that just so far as some men are willing to lend, others will be desirous to borrow; in other words, to whatever extent credit will be given, men can be found desirous of taking it. The consequence is, that where the facilities for contracting debt are unwisely multiplied, a just sense of obligations is lessened, and fraudulent insolvencies generally follow. It is not difficult to see how such a train of evils is to be prevented. No one can borrow if there is no one to lend; and if one man has little motive or inducement to lend, another will have little opportunity or ability to borrow. On this simple principle do we find those laws of the Hebrews constructed which were designed to prevent them from contracting heavy debts. They had their "usury" law, but it was entirely different from ours.* It expressly

* "Usury" means, properly, that which is paid for the use of any thing, whether money, clothing, or whatever one man may lend to another. In this sense it is to be understood in the command, "Thou shalt not lend upon usury to thy brother; usury of money, usury of victuals, or usury of any thing that is lent upon usury. Unto a stranger thou mayest lend upon usury; but unto thy brother thou shalt not lend upon usury." At present, and among us, the word is used to denote exorbitant or unlawful interest on loans of money, being one of many instances which show how the meaning of words is changed with the lapse of time.

forbade one Hebrew to take from another any hire or consideration for the use of money, or other article of value which he might lend. They had also their statute of limitations. It took effect at every Jubilee, when all debts, wherever or however contracted, were cancelled; and then also came the all-important release, which, on that memorable day, restored every one to the landed inheritance of his fathers, freeing it from every claim that any other occupant or cultivator may have previously asserted with regard to it. These being settled and well-known laws respecting the validity of obligations, the creditor could not complain. If he disregarded them the fault was his own; and although in an extensively commercial community such statutes would be deemed too stringent, yet they contain a lesson as to the evil of running into debt, that all men in all pursuits would do well to remember. Especially in an agricultural community they were the life of the people; they saved many an inheritance from being squandered, many a family from being scattered, and many a heart from being broken and driven to despair. And I here take occasion to add that it must give every true philanthropist pleasure to perceive that many of those great principles of wisdom, equity, and mercy, which were embodied in these ordinances of the Hebrew Commonwealth, are becoming more and more understood and brought into notice in our day, though with a difference of form adapted to the present condition of society. In times not long past, creditors who would even act the part of Shylocks, had all in their own way. They could tempt the necessitous into ruinous indebtedness, and then exact the pound of flesh from their unhappy debtor, or doom him to a prison where the whole man was wasted till he sank into the grave. We now consider imprisonment for debt, and which often placed the unfortunate on a level with the criminal, as a remnant of barbarism. The principle involved in the law among the Hebrews, protecting a landed inheritance from perpetual alienation, also begins to be appreciated. A statute has already been adopted by one of our States, and is contemplated by others, which is appropriately entitled "Exemption of the Homestead," as it exempts a man's dwelling from liability on account of his debts, in order that his family may be protected from expulsion and poverty, and that he may himself have a shelter for his own head, while he summons his energies to make further effort for them and for himself. If all our legislatures would adopt some provision like this, which might both mitigate misfortune and hold out encouragement for reformation, the country might, in a great degree, be relieved from that squalid destitution, and despairing helplessness which, from the nature of the case, must be too often encountered in our crowded cities.*

This leads me to notice as another proof of the propitious influence of agriculture upon civil freedom:

Its tendency to produce among a people a *spirit of equality and close sympathy one with another.* Extremes are prone to meet. In our cities we find wealth and poverty, intelligence and ignorance, refinement and debasement, in immediate view of each other; and notwithstanding the philanthropic labors which would bring the abundance of the rich to the relief of the poor, destitution and degradation must remain in painful contrast with luxury and pride. It was an unerring hand that drew, in the picture of Tyre, a description which applies more or less to all our great marts of commerce.—"Thou art a merchant of the people, and art situated at the entry of the sea, and thou hast said I am of perfect beauty.—By thy wisdom, and by thy traffic thou hast increased thy riches, and thine heart is lifted up because of thy riches." Notwithstanding the indispensable importance of our cities for carrying out the great purposes of civilized life, not only as they form the centres of intercourse between

* Note P.

nations, but also give a tone and polish to manners, brighten and invigorate the faculties by the close contact of men with men in their daily pursuits; yet must the great majority of the population, from the very nature of their pursuits, remain so divided from each other as to produce something like a spirit of caste. Buying and selling, the giving of wages and the receiving of wages, which are the principal transactions of city life, place men in an attitude of collision, and create an antagonism of interests which tend to impair sympathy and community of feeling. The prizes in commerce also are comparatively few; while one man rises, other men often sink; and thus is the distance perpetuated which separates one class from another, and shuts out that sentiment of equality which is essential to a well-compacted Republic. For this equality, and the sympathy which grows out of it, we must look among those who are not dependant on the will of another for the employment by which they subsist, but who rely on the soil which they claim as their own, for every thing needful to their comfort and their welfare. The influence of such a position and such occupation in imparting a spirit of independence and self-reliance is seen wherever agriculture is pursued, and is held in merited honor. Though a man cultivates or owns but his hundred, or his fifty acres, he feels that he has rank, and fellowship with his neighbor who may cultivate his thousands. They are both drawn together by a community of employment and of interests that leads them to forget the difference which arises from the mere amount of their respective possessions. Many who now hear me have felt the truth of what I am saying. There are constant examples of it at those annual and praiseworthy assemblages of our agriculturists, where they meet and bring together the choicest productions of their respective fields; the man of affluence, and the man of moderate competency standing side by side with mutual respect and goodwill; he who knows most of agriculture as a science, imparting the fruit of his studies, and he who is best versed in the practice, telling of his experience; both acknowledging the bond that unites them in the cultivation of the earth.

Agriculture also tends *to strengthen the love of a people to their own country.* It must be obvious to every one acquainted with the habits of living and the tenure of property in our cities, that they are not favorable to the growth of strong local attachments. The few square feet occupied by the inhabitant as a home, generally belongs to another, and not to himself; and even where the occupant of a house is its owner, his feelings cannot become bound to its walls by the ties which bind the heart of the husbandman to his fields on which he bestows his careful labor, and which respond to his industry by clothing themselves in the rich beauties of spring, summer and harvest. Especially will these attachments be strengthened if the land which he now possesses has come down to him as an inheritance from his ancestors through generation after generation; and is thus associated with all the feelings of love and reverence with which he cherishes their memories.

There is still another point which should not be overlooked in this connection: I refer to *the healthful sobriety of mind which the occupations and scenes of life in the country are calculated to cherish.* There is quite as much truth as poetry in the words,

"God made the country, man made the town."

And if any one will compare his own feelings when he goes forth among the fields covered with the rich gifts of a Creator's hand, and when again he treads our streets, hemmed in by walls of human workmanship, he will be at no loss to tell in which of the two his mind is rendered most conscious of the presence and authority of the Most High. While Adam yet bore the fresh and unsullied image of his Maker, he was placed in Eden "to dress it and to keep it," as an employment best suited to his state of innocence, and as a means of preserving it. The contemplation of scenes in which "Nature leads up to Nature's God," always tends to impart a tone of moral health, and to form a solidity of character which, especially in a nation enjoying the privilege of self-government, are all important as a balance to the turbulent fervor often generated in our cities. It is in such an atmosphere that the mind is generally most unclouded, and can look beyond the things of a day. Nor should it be forgotten that amidst such scenes and occupations every free nation has found many of her greatest patriots and statesmen.

We might dwell still farther on the effects of agriculture, and of the divine laws respecting it, given to the Hebrews; but enough has been said to show how it was interwoven with their religion as the people of God, and with their freedom as a Commonwealth. Let us now consider how far this feature in their polity and condition was designed to look beyond their land, and to furnish instruction to a nation like our own.

Great principles never change, although the application of them must vary according to varying times and circumstances; and unwise, if not impracticable, as it would be in modern times and among modern nations to adopt the entire system of Hebrew laws respecting the ownership and cultivation of the earth, there is a very instructive lesson to be learned from them respecting the place which should be assigned to agriculture as a source of national prosperity and power in every land. The facilities peculiar to our own country, inviting the mass of the people to this invigorating occupation, have contributed largely to the establishment of her freedom and her growth in power; and because we do not think the merciful ordering of Divine Providence towards our nation in this respect is rightly estimated, we invite your careful attention to it.

The boasted liberty of Greece and of Rome was rather the liberty of a city than of a whole country or nation. Strangers as they were to the principle of representation, through which the sober judgment cherished by a country life could have been brought to keep in check the impetuous ardor of their political assemblies; every great public measure took its direction from the populace who dwelt in the capital. "Hence," as Alison has well remarked, "the violence, the anarchy, and the inconsistency by which their history was so often distinguished, and which, though concealed amid the blaze of ancient eloquence, the searching eye of modern history has so fully illustrated." We could scarcely hope that the liberties enjoyed by our Republic would outlast a single generation in our cities, if they were severed from their political connexion with the country around them. It has often been said, that Paris is France for every political purpose, and this may be one great reason why all their late attempts to acquire freedom have been so abortive in the French nation. The land does not possess an independent intelligent yeomanry to control and moderate the mercurial spirits of her metropolis; and we fully believe that, under God, much of our safety from the evils that are supposed by some to threaten us as a nation is found in the broad expanse of territory which is yet to be improved by the hand of husbandry, and in the growing desire of our own citizens, and of the multitudes that flock to us from abroad, to become owners and tillers of our fruitful soil.

The illustrious Burke, "the unrivalled prophet of politics," as he is sometimes called, described, many years ago, a crowd of American Tartars, armed with the pike and the sabre, pouring from the West over the Alleghanies, and sweeping away the wealth and population of our Eastern cities, grown indolent and defenceless by the natural course of popular government and profligate prosperity. True prophet as that great statesman was when he foretold the results of the French revolution, his wisdom forsook him when he looked towards America. We find more truth and statesman-like sagacity in another distinguished writer, who, although a foreigner, better understood our position and prospects. We also quote him with the more pleasure, for, though it is only about a quarter of a century since he wrote, and his predictions were then considered as uttered in language extravagantly figurative, they are already in process of literal fulfilment. He speaks of "the electric agency of the Post and the Press." The electric spark passing over the wires fulfils his prediction as to the one; and we look for a time not far distant when the same powerful agent will effect a similar improvement in the other. Science has only just begun to discover the value of electricity in promoting the purposes of human life and human improvement. It has already shown that the most rapid movements of the Post in former times were comparatively sluggish. It has now to show that all our past improvements in the art of printing have left it a slow process, when compared with its rapid working after it shall have called to its aid the speed of the lightning.

"The people of the United States," he writes, "find themselves in a condition to devote their whole energies to the cultivation of their vast natural resources. Undisturbed by wars, unburdened by oppressive taxes, unfettered by old prejudices and corruptions; enjoying the united advantages of an infant and a mature society, they are able to apply the highly refined science and art of Europe to the improvement of the virgin soil and unoccupied natural riches of America. They start unincumbered by a thousand evils, political and moral, which weigh down the energies of the old world. The volume of our history lies before them; they may adopt our improvements, avoid our errors, take warning from our sufferings; and, with the combined lights of our experience and their own, build up a more perfect form of society! Even already they have given some momentous and salutary truths to the world. Their rapid growth has first developed the astonishing results of the productive powers of population. We can now calculate with much certainty that America, which yet presents to the eye, generally, the aspect of an untrodden forest, will, in the short space of one century, surpass Europe in the number of its inhabitants. We even hazard little in predicting that before the tide of civilization has rolled back to its original seats, Assyria, Persia, and Palestine, an intelligent population of two or three hundred millions will have overspread the New World, and extended the empire of knowledge and of the arts from Cape Horn to Alaska. Among the vast mass of civilized men, there will be but two languages spoken. The effect of this single circumstance in accelerating the progress of society can scarcely be foreseen. What a field will then be opened to the man of science, the artist, the popular writer who addresses a hundred millions of educated persons! What a stimulus given to mental energy and social improvement, when every useful discovery will be communicated instantaneously to so great a mass of intelligent beings, by the *electric agency of the Post and Press!* Imagination is lost in attempting to estimate the effects of such accumulated means and powers. One result, however, may be anticipated. America must then become the centre of knowledge, civilization and power."

Comparing the views of these two distinguished men, I am reminded of the judicious observation made by a shrewd writer, "that it would have been well for theology if commentators could have been content to take, and not give a meaning, when professing to expound the Sacred Scriptures." It is equally true that it would have been well for the world if statesmen had contented themselves with taking, instead of giving a meaning, when studying the history of nations. And perhaps there is no nation on the face of the earth whose example and position have in this respect been more misunderstood and misrepresented than our own. We can readily account for it. The great questions respecting Church and State, which engage public attention and divide public opinion in Europe, are, in America, brought to the decisive test of experiment; but experiments in civil and ecclesiastical polity are not to be completed with the speedy action of an electric battery. They require time and careful deliberate examination. The causes which are most effectual in producing the final results may, for a long time, be acting with a latent power; and during the process, appearances may be evolved that will lead a hasty and superficial observer to conclusions directly at variance with what may be found in the end to be truth and reality. Indeed, it is generally seen that the most valuable results are those which require the most time, and pass through the greatest variety of changes, before they are fully developed. When our fruit trees are in bloom, an observer, who is a stranger to their nature, might suppose that they were designed to answer the same end with the violet, the rose and the lily, to produce their flower and nothing more; but if he waits, he will find that the blossom was only an incipient form in which the life of the tree displayed itself, and in which it made preparation for the growth and maturity of the nutricious fruit.

Much, if not the whole of this seems to be forgotten by several political economists abroad, who take opposite sides on the questions which they seek to determine by what is occurring in this country. They act with the hot haste of the empiric who will seize upon every new and imperfect result and try to force it into the support of his own favorite theory. This unphilosophic and selfish determination to bend facts into a correspondence with foregone conclusions, instead of drawing conclusions from facts deliberately weighed after they have been fairly ascertained, has led many able men abroad into most strange, if not ridiculous mistakes. They would build for America with the square, and compass, and plumb line of Europe; and when they find any divergence from their rules of beauty and stability, they condemn the edifice as raised in ignorance and doomed to early ruin. They forget that many of the usages in both Church and State, which might have been wise centuries ago, are now to be viewed as obsolete and behind the age. They seem as if they had yet to learn that there are sources of good working their way in the New World which were never felt in the Old; and that there are causes of suffering and evil in the Old that have no existence in the New.

To refer to the predictions of Burke. We reply to it, that the spirit of the Tartars has never emigrated to the Western Hemisphere. It cannot take root in a region like this. The natural and constant course of events with us is directly the reverse of the aims and achievements of Tartar hordes rushing down from their wilds to ravage states and cities grown weak and effeminate by luxury and indolence. Our elder states and cities do not grow defenceless or weak, as he supposed, by the natural course of popular government and long prosperity. Our far west is not left to be a barren wild, occupied only by barbarians, savage and untamed. On the contrary, our own people from our Eastern States, and thousands upon thousands from our Eastern Hemisphere are pouring year after year into that vast wilderness, and subduing the rich soil to the purposes of civilization and refinement. There is no war waged upon the older states by marauders pouring down from the Alleghanies, with pike and sabre to plunder and pillage the wealth and luxuries they could not find at home. But the invasion is from the older States upon the new; and the only war carried on, is with the wilderness, with the forest, and with the unreclaimed prairie. Instead of the invaders leaving behind them, and on their path, desolation, such as marked the way of Tartars, Goths or Vandals; their progress is known by "the wilderness becoming a fruitful field," and the evidences of a wealth which they had not wrested from others, but created for themselves. They are opening and widening the resources of new States, which, instead of abstracting from the wealth and safety of the old, afford them a prop and means of recovery, when the convulsions of commerce may have shattered their strength and impaired their resources.

It cannot fail to be seen that in these peculiar features of our country the Great Disposer of events has rendered agriculture a leading and prominent employment in America, as he formerly made it in Palestine. THERE he established this order of things by express laws. HERE he has done it by the decree and the movements of his Providence. We cannot change it if we would; and if we rightly understand our own welfare as a free nation, we would not change it if we could. The wisest and greatest of philanthropists and statesmen abroad see its results, and are now taking lessons of wisdom for themselves from our experience. To quote once more from one of them who may well be ranked among the most able men of our age;—

"America," he has recently said, "America seems to have been reserved as a land of experiment for these latter times, a vast field in which all the lessons essential to the prosperity of Europe may be exhibited to the eye of nations. The first lesson is given in its agriculture. The husbandmen of America are shown to be the true strength of the country;

it is the culture of the earth that the State falls back upon in all its difficulties. All the showy expedients for fabricating wealth out of nothing, which are so familiar in Europe, are there proved to be fallacies on the largest scale of demonstration. Trading without capital, and currency without specie, are the two grand charlatanries of the world. America has tried them both, and again and again has seen her thousands utterly ruined. Yet all this passes by; the land again brings forth her produce; the strong husbandman props up the shattered merchant —the State, like a sickly patient, recovers by the diet of the farm. The country has such a mine of wealth in the soil, such facilities for recovery in the plough and the spade, such endless storehouses of national wealth in the forest, the prairie, and the mountain, that the commercial ruin is no more felt than the peasant feels the mouldering of the leaves which fell in the last autumn, and which are at the moment preparing a new fertility for the soil."*

The picture can hardly be said to be too highly colored. It recals to our minds occasions of commer-

* In some of the preceding paragraphs I have used the language of distinguished writers abroad, the more freely in order to show that these views respecting the resources and prospects of America are not confined to Americans. The estimate of our country by statesmen in Europe has been greatly and justly changed within the last few years.

cial distress which are of too frequent occurrence; and when we look back to the times in which we have seen fortunes wrecked, hearts broken; and sometimes honesty violated, honor lost, and the grave left as the only hiding place from the storm; we would raise the voice of warning to the youth of our country against the too prevalent desire for rushing into the marts of commerce, and neglecting, or undervaluing the noble occupation of tilling the earth. Ardent haste is the attribute of youth, whether it be in a young man or in a young nation; and the "haste to become rich" by a successful adventure that would accomplish all in a day, and not by the patient labor of a life, is the besetting sin of many in our youthful nation. It leads them too often to look on the labors of husbandry as tame, spiritless and unpromising; and to rush with inconsiderate ambition into our large cities, which have often proved a vast Maelstrom to the hopes and the lives of those who would have met with a different end had they called their energies into action in a different sphere.

As a remedy for this too prevalent tendency, let us ask, have the public authorities of the land done their duty to put honor on agriculture, and to render it attractive as an employment leading to both profit and distinction? Although we have a soil of such variety and richness, that it might reward the hand of industry with every product that can minister to health or comfort, its fertility has never been fairly tested. Our experiments are yet merely on the surface. The wealth that lies beneath remains to be explored and developed; and to accomplish this great end adequately and successfully, we need something more than the industry of individuals. We need instruction in agriculture as a profession. We need agricultural schools or colleges, to teach how science can be applied to develope and improve the riches of the earth. Every State in the nation should found and endow them either as independent and separate institutions, or as distinct departments of institutions already existing. They would scatter their benefits broadcast over the land, adding to the public wealth, and giving to the agriculturist his share in the improved intelligence of our day. He is now often left to work in the dark, to spend labor in vain which adequate instruction would enable him to render doubly available. It is due also to science that she should now have an opportunity both to vindicate her claims to public favor and to redeem lost time. In former ages of the world she confined herself to the cloister. She seemed to fear that her dignity and delicacy would suffer by allowing the sweet air of the fields to breathe upon her cheek, or by lending her aid to any of the practical pursuits of life. She has become wearied of an existence both sickly and useless; and now comes forth and goes about doing good, gaining strength and brightness from her active labors. She has given skill and success to the mechanic, the manufacturer, and the mariner; and she waits to pour her wealth of knowledge into the ear of the husbandman, to lessen the weight of his toil, and yet give him a richer harvest. Little as she has yet been allowed to do for him, compared with her power and her will to serve him, she has already so improved his implements that he can accomplish in an hour an amount of service that would once have consumed whole days. She has discovered to him mines of wealth in what he once considered as wastes and blemishes on the earth. She has taught him that the marsh once dreaded as a source of disease and suffering to himself, may be converted into the means of fertilizing his fields; and that much of what he once labored to cast away as refuse and loss, are his best sources of gain, the means which nature provides for the restoration of her own exhausted energies. Did we only understand the wise economy of the Creator throughout the whole of his works, we would see how carefully he has framed his laws to gather up the "fragments that nothing be lost."

One great end of modern discoveries is to show how this may be done, how everything may be turned to wise account in promoting the comfort and benefit of man. Let science do her appropriate work for the husbandman, and the very desert would be converted into a fruitful field. The wilds that have lain for ages as blots on the page of nature, are a reproach to man, not to his Maker—a proof of our want of knowledge, not of His want of wisdom and mercy. His "goodness is over all His works," and we owe it alike to Him and to ourselves that we should be enabled to appreciate the wise bounty of his hand, and improve it for the benefit of our race. And while this should be viewed as the duty of all civilized nations, it becomes especially important in a country like ours, where husbandry is not only the great means of providing for the wants of life, but is also interwoven with the preservation of our civil freedom.

In drawing the whole subject to a conclusion, we observe that, highly as we ought to value civil freedom, we should be careful not to expect too much from it. It is not a panacea for every ill of life. "I have seen an end of all perfection," says the Psalmist, and he had not to go far in order to find it. It would meet his eye in every thing which belongs to earth and time. All government, whether devised or administered by man, must have its imperfections; and the forgetfulness of this plain truth creates in the minds of many a spirit of ingratitude and discontent. They would treat our government as the heathens treat some of their idols. When every thing is bright and prosperous they exalt it to the skies; but when public disasters or times of trial come they turn round and revile what they had previously idolized. In our fallen world evil is so universally mingled with good that we have but a choice between evils; and our wisdom is shown by contentment with benefits in which the least amount of evil is mingled with the greatest amount of good. The history of all nations, whether ancient or modern, shows that there is no depositary of political power where it is not liable to abuse; and the perfection of wise statemanship is seen in placing it where it may be more securely guarded, or where abuse, if committed, may be so restricted as to be least injurious to the people.

Our government proceeds on the principle that power is best guarded when placed in the hands of the people themselves, for if wrong is done they are the first to feel it, and will be most anxious to remedy it. But if public measures are to be submitted to the public voice, we must expect to see clamor and strife when the freedom of public opinion and public discussion have arrayed party against party. If we are protected from the tyranny of power in the hands of one or a few whose will is law, we must exercise a constant vigilance over ourselves and others, that the great principles of liberty and equality suffer no violation. If we are safe from the exactions to which the subject must submit to gratify the ambition or pride of royalty, we must also be ready of our own accord at times to sacrifice something of our own ease, perhaps also of our own interests, in order to promote and preserve the good of the Commonwealth. Such is the price which must be paid for the enjoyment of civil freedom, and they who think the price of more value than the prize must seek relief where the people do not bear rule.

In viewing our condition as a Republic, we should keep in mind that the government with us is better or worse just according as "we, the people," choose to make it the one or the other; and it is generally found that those who complain most, are the very men who do the least to rectify the evils from which they profess to be suffering. The ballot-box, the election of the rulers by the ruled, is our great means of redress against public wrongs, our great means of effecting whatever is most conducive to public good. It is an essential feature in the structure of civil freedom, which gives vitality and stability to the whole. But how many talk loudly respecting the right of suffrage, who never seem to have reflected on the duty of suffrage; and as an excuse for their neglect, they will plead that they wish to have nothing to do with politics? If by this vague expression they mean that they will not mingle in the bitter strifes of party, that they will not join in measures foul and dishonest for hunting down the reputation of an opposite candidate, that they will enter into no corrupting combination to delude the public mind—then, they are right in having nothing to do with politics. But if they mean by it that they will be at no pains to consult with the wise and the good as to what may be for the welfare of their country; that they will put themselves to no inconvenience in order to see that "able men" are presented to the people for office; that they will not spare time from their business to exercise their right of suffrage on behalf of such candidates when offered; then, if they will have nothing to do with politics, the time may soon come when they and their children can have nothing to do with freedom. Let sober and intelligent citizens indulge such supineness, and the consequence is both plain and inevitable. Our free institutions must fall into the hands of the depraved and worthless, to be perverted to public injury, if not to public ruin.

We speak without reference to party. The faults may be equally chargeable upon men of all parties in the State. We allude to every member of the Commonwealth who enjoys protection from the government. It is a duty which he owes to himself, to his country, and to his Maker, to inform himself in matters of public interest, and to act according to the best light he can gain.

Treason is not to be feared in a nation like ours while the friends of freedom and good order are awake to their duty, and on the alert to fulfil it. It was "while men slept that the enemy came and sowed tares among the wheat." And if men who possess integrity and intelligence will not bring their aid to the support and defence of the national privileges which they inherit from their fathers, they will find, when too late, that they have sold their birthright for a price more shameful than a mess of pottage—for the indulgence of their own ease; and that freedom may be lost by their own fault as irretrievably as if wrested from them by the hand of some overpowering usurper. Every man should remember that his influence, whether in Church or State, is felt for good or for evil. It is a talent, however small he may esteem it, which he is not at liberty to "keep laid up in a napkin;" and he is one day to be called to account for its improvement.

There is still another concluding observation which we would urge with much earnestness on the minds of rulers and ruled. It is our great responsibility as a Republic. We hold our free institutions as a trust from the Most High God, not only for the benefit of ourselves and our children, but of all the oppressed nations of the earth.

When the United Provinces of the Netherlands had commenced their struggles for independence, the first coin which they issued bore the emblem of a vessel at sea struggling with the waves, without either sail or oar, and with the motto, "Incertum quo fata ferunt." Complicated and appalling as were the disadvantages with which Holland had to struggle in her noble effort for freedom, and doubtful at the first as she deemed the result, had she been overpowered in the end her fall would not have closed the door of hope against other nations. They might still have been encouraged to aspire after freedom, when they could have unfurled her banner under better auspices. But if free institutions cannot be maintained in this country, what is left for others to expect? Must they not conclude that, after all, a republic is more of a name than a reality; rather a Utopian dream than a substantial and practicable good? If with our advantages, as we have described them, of geographical position, of general intelligence and enlightened Christianity, civil freedom is not to be preserved in our land, is she not to be viewed like the dove of the patriarch, as barely hovering over a world so covered with a deluge of ruin and a strife of elements as to allow her no resting place for the sole of her foot?

The nation should then view herself as "a city set upon a hill, that cannot be hid." If the experiment of free government fails in our hands, our fall brings down with it the hopes of the world. The eyes of multitudes, who are suffering bondage and oppression, are fixed upon us with the conviction that the issue with us determines the future for them. It is our destiny either to be the deep grave where their hopes are to be entombed in darkness, or the brightening pillar of light that shall invite them from bondage to liberty and peace.

Such a responsibility, although sublime and inspiriting, carries with it consequences that are exceedingly solemn. We feel that He "who ruleth over the kingdoms of the earth," has called us to bear it; and the banner of the nation seems to remind us that the founders of our Republic assumed it deliberately, and with high yet humble confidence as to the result.

They chose as the national emblem, not a vessel struggling with the waves, without sail or oar, but the eagle on outspread wings ready either to face the storm or soar above it, bearing in its beak the motto, "E pluribus unum," as the foundation on which, under God, they built their trust. And to the Union, the integrity and perpetuity of the Union among the States, rendering the confederacy "one and indivisible, now and for ever," the statesmen who wear their mantle still look as the source of our strength and our prosperity. The Union is to Liberty like the fabled Cestus, or zone of Venus, giving symmetry, beauty, life, and finish to the whole form; while without it, all is imperfection, disorder, and exposure. It is the very point of public welfare which the acknowledged Father of his country seems to have touched with a tremulous hand in his last farewell, as he brought to view the dangers that might assail us when he should be in his grave. Indeed, in that memorable address, which breathes throughout the anxieties of a parental regard, it seems to have dwelt on his mind as a grateful and hallowed recollection, that when he and his compatriots gave us freedom and independence as our heritage, they gave us also "the United States" as a name by which we should first be known among nations; trusting that, having borne it from infancy, we would look upon every attempt to efface it from the national escutcheon as both profanity and treason. As we have received it thus solemnly consecrated to our keeping, were we now to throw it away, or allow it to be lost, we would bring upon ourselves not only a misfortune, but a guilt against God and man which might justly be punished in torrents of blood, and in the end by a grinding despotism sought as the only relief from the sword of civil war.

But notwithstanding the excitement of debate, and the irritation arising from actual wrongs, we cannot persuade ourselves that the nation is ever to become so lost to her own welfare, and the welfare of the world, as to allow her noble confederacy to be rent asunder and destroyed. The union of the United States in America does not depend, as did the union of the tribes among the Hebrews, on the wayward and unfeeling tyranny of a king refusing all due concessions to the demands of justice. It was created in a spirit of compromise and concession among States equally sovereign, whether small or great; it was prompted by a sense then deeply felt of the danger to all if there was not a union of all; and we fully believe that, with the blessing of the Most High, which has hitherto followed us, by a like spirit of moderation and good will, and by a scrupulous care to preserve inviolate the ancient landmarks of the federacy, the Union will still be maintained. Its strength has already, and more than once, been tried by strong disturbing forces; and prophets of evil have arisen, both at home and abroad, who have foretold a disastrous issue. We have outlived both them and their predictions. The confederation is still unbroken, and general attachment to it is strengthened, rather than weakened, by every trial to which it has been subjected. Such occasions turn the thoughts of the people to consider anew its vast importance. The more carefully they contemplate it, the more highly do they value it; and as time rolls on, adding to its age, they regard it with increased veneration. More than all, it is sustained by a common religious faith, which of itself would be a powerful restraint against the commencement of a strife in which brother would be required to turn his hand against brother. Then also, the whole land is now feeling more and more the moral power of the railroad and the telegraph, which create throughout its most distant extremities the sympathies of close neighborhood.

And here we think is found a great security against the alarm which many have felt from the enlargement of the national territory. No one can suppose that we are less united because we have grown beyond "the old Thirteen," and embrace in our Union the States lying in the wide valley of the Mississippi and on the shores of our ocean-like Western Lakes. The result of this growth, which has added to the grandeur of the national edifice, has increased instead of impairing its strength and stability. Experience has thus far shown, that the federative bond was formed to comprehend a great nation; that it has a power of expansion and adaptation not fully understood in the early history of the country. Diversified as the various States may have become in climate, interests, and tastes, it leaves them "ample room and verge enough" for free and independent action on whatever immediately concerns themselves, while it unites and binds them under one government only so far as is required for the safety and welfare of the whole. Wise observers of our past progress, contemplating it from abroad, have remarked, "The wider the dominion of the federation spreads, the greater the number of local interests and populations comprehended within its boundary, the less appears to be the probability that any particular local interest can threaten the general weal—that dissensions between particular sections are destined to endanger the security of the Union." A cause of disturbance that might lash into a foam the whole waters of a small lake, would not be felt in the greater depths and wider extent of an ocean.

And now, when of late the nation has spread itself over a region so wide as might once have rendered the people strangers to each other through the vast distance between them, and thus have prepared the way for their political severance; we have, as a new gift from Heaven, sent just at the right season for our wants, these new and rapid means of communication which are destined to create a new era in unity of sentiment and interest between man and man, and which already are fast tesselating our continent from shore to shore, and binding its inhabitants together in a network of iron and steel. Wide then as our country may spread, even were "the whole continent ours," as to moral and political purposes distance is annihilated. The Atlantic and Pacific are now neighboring oceans. The Hudson and the Columbia are as near to each other as were the Hudson and the Delaware thirty years ago.

We love to look at the workings of these new agencies, and to see how they harmonize without destroying that diversity of character among our citizens which arises from difference of climate and pursuit; and which we deem an essential element of our rising greatness. If a body is complete in symmetry and strength, all the members must not be cast in the same mould. As Paul says in another case, "The body is not one member, but many. If the whole body were the eye, where were the hearing? If the whole body were the hearing, where were the smelling?" The principle is the same in all well-compacted bodies of men. An uniform sameness in the materials of national character renders it tame. The whole framework of the Commonwealth is invigorated and stands out in bolder relief, when it brings into harmonious combination those great and discriminating features which now distinguish one section of her people from the others; and were they obliterated, it would be her loss rather than her gain. Nor in all the collisions which may arise from a prevailing diversity of views, feelings, and condition, do we see any thing which, under the control of wise statesmen, cannot be merged in national sympathies and efficient co-operation for the general welfare.*

We have dwelt the more fully on the danger to the Union, which is supposed by many to arise from the extension of the national boundaries, because it so occupies their minds as to divert their attention from what we consider as the great source of apprehension. The delusion would be pregnant with

* Note O

calamity to our country if she was either to believe that she is secure against all harm, or to overlook the danger which is most imminent and serious. This fair tree may be spreading its branches over the length and the breadth of the land, and yet there may be a worm at the root. Our great danger is from the spread of corruption among the people—among the people, I repeat—for if the people remain sound and true to themselves; should rulers become faithless to their trust, they would be hurled from their places before their traitorous hand could touch the life-spring of the Commonwealth. Our government is too safely guarded by checks and balances to leave any scope for the ambitious designs of usurpation. If the nation is ever destroyed it must be the work of self-destruction. If she falls it must be by her own hand. If she stands she must be true to herself, and to that allegiance to Heaven in which she was trained by her founders when they raised her to independence. Nothing but a high and pervading sense of moral obligation, such as can spring only from an enlightened Christianity predominating among all ranks, and through all diversities of clime and character, can preserve from generation to generation the blessings of such freedom as we enjoy. It is our deep conviction of this truth which has led us, in these Lectures, to present the leading principles of free civil government in a light which may prove that the Bible, the Holy Bible, "known and read of all men," is the last but sure hope of America.

THE END.

NOTES.

NOTE A.—Lecture 1. p. 26.

The Journal of Congress shows how carefully the founders of our Republic cherished a deep sense of their dependance on God, and how highly they valued the Scriptures and the ordinances of Christianity as essential to the welfare of the nation.

During the Revolution there was a painful scarcity of Bibles throughout the country. Few, if any, were imported, and booksellers had not the capital and other means for publishing an American edition. The subject was brought before Congress, and was referred to a Committee, who gave it their careful attention. On the 11th of September, 1777, they reported to the House:—

"That they have conferred fully with the printers, &c. in this city, and are of opinion, that the proper types for printing the Bible are not to be had in this country, and that the paper cannot be procured, but with such difficulties, and subject to such casualties, as render any dependence on it altogether improper; that to import types for the purpose of setting up an entire edition of the Bible, and to strike off 30,000 copies, with paper, binding, &c. will cost £10,272 10s., which must be advanced by Congress, to be reimbursed by the sale of the books; that, in the opinion of the Committee, considerable difficulties will attend the procuring the types and paper; that afterwards the risk of importing them will considerably enhance the cost, and that the calculations are subject to such uncertainty in the present state of affairs, that Congress cannot much rely on them; that the use of the Bible is so universal, and its importance so great, that your Committee refer the above to the consideration of Congress, and if Congress shall not think it expedient to order the importation of types and paper, the Committee recommend that Congress will order the Committee of Commerce to import 20,000 Bibles from Holland, Scotland, or elsewhere, into the different States of the Union."

"Whereupon," adds the Journal, "it was moved, That the Committee of Commerce be directed to import 20,000 copies of the Bible; and it was resolved in the affirmative."

We may better understand the "great importance" which Congress attached to the Bible, if we recollect that when they passed this resolution appropriating funds for the proposed importation, they were greatly pressed by the want of money in the Treasury for the support of their troops then in the field.

This Christian spirit is also very clearly exhibited in the frequency with which Congress appointed days of fasting, humiliation and prayer, and also seasonable days of thanksgiving during the whole period of the Revolutionary struggle. The language used in their various proclamations shows that they were not ashamed or afraid to speak plainly on the great truths of Christianity. When it was perceived in the early part of the year 1776, that war was inevitable, they issued the following recommendation:—

"In times of impending calamity and distress, when the liberties of America are imminently endangered by the secret machinations and open assaults of an insidious and vindictive administration, it becomes the indispensable duty of these hitherto free and happy Colonies, with true penitence of heart, and the most reverent devotion, publicly to acknowledge the over-ruling providence of God; to confess and deplore our offences against him, and to supplicate his interposition for averting the threatened danger, and prospering our strenuous efforts in the cause of freedom, virtue and posterity.

"The Congress, therefore, considering the warlike preparations of the British Ministry to subvert our invaluable rights and privileges, and to reduce us by fire and sword, by the savages of the wilderness and our own domestics, to the most abject and ignominious bondage; desirous, at the same time, to have people of all ranks and degrees duly impressed with a solemn sense of God's superintending providence, and of their duty duly to rely in all their lawful enterprises on his aid and direction, do earnestly recommend that Friday, the 17th day of May next, be observed by the said Colonies as a day of humiliation, fasting and prayer, that we may, with united hearts, confess and bewail our manifold sins and transgressions, and by a sincere repentance and amendment of life, appease His righteous displeasure, and through the mediation of Jesus Christ, obtain his pardon and forgiveness, humbly imploring his assistance to frustrate the cruel purposes of our unnatural enemies, and by inclining their hearts to justice and benevolence, prevent the further effusion of kindred blood. But if, continuing deaf to the voice of reason and humanity, and inflexibly bent on desolation and war, they constrain us to repel their hostile invasion by open resistance, that it may please the Lord of Hosts, the God of Armies, to animate our officers and soldiers with invincible fortitude, to guard and protect them in the day of battle, and to crown the Continental Army, by sea and by land, with victory and success; earnestly beseeching him to bless our civil rulers and representatives of the people in their several assemblies and conventions; to preserve and strengthen their union, to give wisdom and stability to their councils, and direct them to the most efficacious measures for establishing the rights of America on the most honorable and permanent basis; that He would be graciously pleased to bless all his people in these Colonies with health and plenty, and grant that a spirit of incorruptible patriotism, and of pure, undefiled religion may universally prevail, and this Continent be speedily restored to the blessings of peace and liberty, and enabled to transmit them inviolate to the latest posterity. And it is recommended to Christians of all denominations to assemble for public worship, and abstain from servile labor on the said day."

We have not space to quote all the proclamations which were issued during the war, appointing days either of humiliation or thanksgiving. But we will make room for the two following; the first of which was adopted in October,

1779, after several instances of success had attended the American army, and is as follows :—

"Whereas it becomes us humbly to approach the Throne of Almighty God, with gratitude and praise for the wonders which His goodness has wrought in conducting our forefathers to this Western World; for his protection to them and to their posterity amidst difficulties and dangers; for raising us, their children, from deep distress to be numbered among the nations of the earth, and for arming the hands of just and mighty princes in our deliverance; and especially for that He hath been pleased to grant us the enjoyment of health, and so to order the revolving seasons that the earth hath produced her increase in abundance, blessing the labors of the husbandman and spreading plenty through the land; that He hath prospered our arms and those of our ally; been a shield to our troops in the hour of danger, pointed their swords to victory, and led them in triumph over the bulwarks of the foe; that He hath gone with those who went out into the wilderness against the savage tribes; that He hath stayed the hand of the spoiler, and turned back his meditated destruction; that He hath prospered our commerce, and given success to those who fought the enemy on the face of the deep; and, above all, that he hath diffused the glorious light of the Gospel, whereby, through the merits of our gracious Redeemer, we may become the heirs of his eternal glory: therefore,

"*Resolved,* That it be recommended to the several States to appoint Thursday, the 9th of December next, to be a day of public and solemn thanksgiving to Almighty God for His mercies, and of prayer for the continuance of His favor and protection to these United States; to beseech Him that He would be graciously pleased to influence our public councils, and bless them with wisdom from on high, with unanimity, firmness and success; that He would go forth with our hosts and crown our armies with victory; that He would grant to his church the plentiful effusion of divine grace, and pour out his Holy Spirit on all ministers of the Gospel; that He would bless and prosper the means of education, and spread the light of Christian knowledge through the remotest corners of the earth; that He would smile upon the labors of His people, and cause the earth to bring forth her fruits in abundance, that we may with gratitude and gladness enjoy them; that He would take under His holy protection our illustrious ally, give him victory over his enemies, and render him signally great as the father of his people and the protector of the rights of mankind; that He would be graciously pleased to turn the hearts of our enemies, and to dispense the blessings of peace to contending nations; that he would in mercy look down upon us, pardon our sins, and receive us into His favor, and finally, that he would establish the independence of these United States upon the basis of religion and virtue, and support and protect them in the enjoyment of peace, liberty and safety."

When intelligence was received that the British Army had capitulated at Yorktown, it was immediately

"*Resolved*, that Congress will at 2 o'clock this day go in procession to the Dutch Lutheran Church, and return thanks to Almighty God for crowning the allied arms of the United States and France with success, by the surrender of the whole British Army under the command of the Earl Cornwallis."

The same devout spirit had been manifested in the army itself. The day after the surrender, General Washington issued an order which closes in the following words:—

"Divine service shall be performed to-morrow in the different brigades and divisions. The Commander-in-Chief recommends that all the troops that are not upon duty, do assist at it with a serious deportment, and that sensibility of heart which the recollection of the surprising and particular interposition of Providence in our favor claims."

The auspicious event was commended as a subject of thankfulness to the whole nation in the following proclamation:—

"Whereas, it hath pleased Almighty God, the Father of Mercies, remarkably to assist and support the United States of America in their important struggle for liberty, against the long continued efforts of a powerful nation, it is the duty of all ranks to observe and thankfully to acknowledge the interposition of his providence in their behalf. Through the whole of the contest, from its first rise to this time, the influence of Divine Providence may be clearly perceived in many signal instances, of which we mention but a few.

"In revealing the councils of our enemies, when the discoveries were seasonable and important, and the means seemingly inadequate or fortuitous; in preserving and even improving the union of the several States, on the breach of which our enemies place their greatest dependence; in increasing the number and adding to the zeal and attachment of the friends of liberty; in granting remarkable deliverances, and blessing us with the most signal success when affairs seemed to have the most discouraging appearance; in raising up for us a powerful and generous ally in one of the first of the European powers; in confounding the councils of our enemies, and suffering them to pursue such measures as have most directly contributed to frustrate their own desires and expectations; above all, in making their extreme cruelty to the inhabitants of these States when in their power, and their savage devastation of property, the very means of cementing our union, and adding vigor to every effort in opposition to them.

"And as we cannot help leading the good people of these States to a retrospect of the events which have taken place since the beginning of the war, so we recommend in a particular manner to their observation, the goodness of God in the year now drawing to a conclusion; in which the confederation of the United States has been completed; in which there has been so many instances of prowess and success in our armies, particularly in the Southern States, where, notwithstanding the difficulties with which they had to struggle, they have recovered the whole country which the enemy had overrun, leaving them only a post or two on or near the sea; in which we have been so powerfully and effectually assisted by our allies, while in all the conjunct operations the most perfect harmony has subsisted in the allied army; in which there has been so plentiful a harvest and so great abundance of the fruits of the earth of every kind, as not only enables us easily to supply the wants of our army, but gives comfort and happiness to the whole people; and, in which, after the success of our allies by sea, a general of the first rank, with his whole army, has been captured by the allied forces under the direction of our Commander-in-Chief.

"It is therefore recommended to the several States to set

apart the 13th day of December next, to be religiously observed as a day of thanksgiving and prayer; that all the people may assemble on that day, with grateful hearts, to celebrate the praises of our Gracious Benefactor; to confess our manifold sins; to offer up our most fervent supplications to the God of all grace, that it may please Him to pardon our offences, and incline our hearts for the future to keep all his laws; to comfort and relieve all our brethren who are in distress or captivity; to prosper our husbandmen, and give success to all engaged in lawful commerce; to impart wisdom and integrity to our counsellors, judgment and fortitude to our officers and soldiers; to protect and prosper our illustrious ally, and favor our united exertions for the speedy establishment of a safe, honorable and lasting peace; to bless all seminaries of learning, and cause the knowledge of God to cover the earth, as the waters cover the seas."

It is refreshing to the Christian patriot to find such sentiments avowed so fully and cordially by the fathers of our Republic in their public acts and proceedings. They had no relish for that diluted and meagre Christianity which is too nearly allied to a refined Paganism; but they speak out the truths of the Bible, and in the language of the Bible, as men who believed in them and gloried in them.

NOTE B.—Lecture 2. p. 59.

I refer to Alison. In the introduction to his History of Europe, having spoken of the overthrow of the Roman Empire, he proceeds to say:—

"But the conquests of the Northern nations led to one important consequence—the establishment of representative governments in the provinces of the empire. The liberty of antiquity cradled in single cities, was confined to the citizens who were present on the spot, and could take an active part in the public deliberations. Though the Romans, with unexampled wisdom, extended the rights of citizenship to the conquered provinces, yet the idea of admitting them to a share of the representation never occurred to their minds; and the more important privileges of a citizen could only be exercised by actually repairing to the metropolis. The unavoidable consequence of this was, that the populace of the capital, in all the free states of antiquity, exercised the principal powers of government; from their passions the public measures took their rise, and by their tumults revolutions in the state were effected. Hence the violence, the anarchy, and the inconstancy by which their history was so often distinguished, and which, though concealed amid the blaze of ancient eloquence, the searching eye of modern history has so fully illustrated.

"The northern nations on the other hand, who established themselves on the ruins of the Roman Empire, were actuated by different feelings and influenced by opposite habits. The liberty which they brought with them from their woods, or which had sprung up amidst the independence of the desert, knew no locality, and was confined to no district. The whole nation was originally free, and that freedom was equally preserved and valued in the cultivated plain as in the desert wilds. * * * It was the discovery of rich and cultivated districts, tenanted by a skilful but unwarlike people, which encouraged the rural settlement of the conquerors, which rendered the protection of cities unnecessary and provided a counterpoise to their allurements; and by establishing the invaders in a permanent manner in the country, long preserved their manners from corruption, and rendered the servitude of the Roman Empire one remote cause of the liberty of modern Europe.

"On the first settlement of the victorious nations, the popular assemblies of the soldiers were an actual convocation of the military array of the kingdoms. William the Conqueror summoned his whole military followers to assemble at Winchester, and sixty thousand men obeyed the mandate, the poorest of whom held property adequate to the maintenance of a horseman and his attendants. The meetings of the *Champs-de-Mai* were less a deputation from the followers of Clovis, than an actual congregation of their numbers in one vast assembly. But, in process of time, the burden of travelling from a distance was severely felt, and the prevalence of sedentary habits rendered the landed proprietors unwilling to undertake the risk or expense of personal attendance on the great council of the state. Hence the introduction of *Parliaments* or *Representative Legislatures*, the greatest addition to the cause of liberty which modern times has afforded; which combine the energy of a democratic with the caution of an aristocratic government; which temper the turbulence and allay the fervor of cities by the slowness and tenacity of country life, and which, when the balance is duly preserved in the composition of the assembly, provide in the variety of its interests and habits, a permanent check upon the violence or injustice of a part of its members.

"It is doubtful, however, whether these causes, powerful as they are, would have led to the introduction of that great and hitherto unknown change in government which the representative system introduced, had not a model existed for imitation, in which for a series of ages, it had been fully established. The councils of the church had so early as the sixth century introduced over all christendom the most perfect system of representation. Delegates from the most remote dioceses in Europe and Asia had there assembled to deliberate on the concerns of the faithful, and every Christian priest, in the humblest station, had some share in the formation of those great assemblies, by whom the general affairs of the church were to be regulated. The formation of parliaments, under the representative system, took place in all the European States in the thirteenth and fourteenth centuries. The industry of antiquarians may carry the Wittenagemot or actual Assembly of leading men a few generations further back; but six centuries before, the Councils of Nice and Antioch had exhibited perfect models of an universal system of representation, embracing a wider sphere than the whole extent of the Roman Empire. There can be no doubt that it was this example, so generally known, and of such powerful authority, which determined the imitation of the other members of the community, where they had any common concerns which required deliberation, and thus to the other blessings which civilization owes to Christianity are to be added those inestimable advantages which have flowed from the establishment of the representative system."

Brougham, in his valuable work entitled "Political Philosophy," claims "the representative principle as the great invention of modern times;" but admits that the "Commonwealths of antiquity made so near an approach to it, as leaves us in some wonder how they never should have made that important step in the art of government." He refers to the Republics of Greece and others, in which the choice of rulers was often submitted to the blind hazard of the lot, and not to the intelligent and deliberate action of the people. Had he turned to the Commonwealth of the Hebrews, he might have there found everything that he has defined as essential to Representation. It is not a little strange that such men as Alison, Brougham and others, in their extensive researches on such subjects, should so entirely overlook what is contained in the Bible respecting the great principles which enter into the constitution of civil government.

NOTE C.—Lecture 2, p. 59

From the various Commentaries which show how the passages in Exodus and Deuteronomy are to be reconciled, I will quote the Exposition by Graves, cited in the Comprehensive Commentary. He observes, on the narrative in Deuteronomy:—

"There is a great and striking difference betwixt this statement and that of Exodus, 18 : 17–22, but no contradiction. Jethro suggested to Moses the appointment. He, probably after consulting God, as Jethro intimates—'If God shall command thee so,' Exodus, 18 : 23, referred the matter to the people, and assigned the choice of the individuals to them; the persons thus selected he admitted to share his authority, as subordinate judges. Thus the two statements are perfectly consistent. But this is not all: their difference is most natural. In first recording the event, it was natural for Moses to dwell on the first cause which led to it, and pass by the appeal to the people as a subordinate and less material part of the transaction; but in addressing the people, it was natural to notice the part they themselves had in the selection of those judges, in order to conciliate their regard and obedience. How naturally, also, does this pious legislator, in his public address, dwell on every circumstance which could improve his hearers in piety and virtue! The multitude of the people was the cause of the appointment of the Judges. How beautifully is this increase of the nation turned to an argument of gratitude to God! How admirably does he take occasion, from mentioning the Judges, to inculcate the eternal principles of justice and piety which should control their decisions! How remote is all this from art, forgery, imposture! Surely here, if anywhere, we can trace the dictates of nature, truth, and piety."

NOTE D.—Lecture 2, p. 64.

"From various passages of the Pentateuch, we find that Moses, at making known any laws, had to convene the whole congregation of Israel (קהל or עדה); and, in like manner, in the Book of Joshua, we see, that when Diets were held, the whole congregation were assembled. If on such occasions every individual had to give his vote, everything would certainly have been democratic in the highest degree; but it is scarcely conceivable how, without any particular regulations made for the purpose, (which, however, we nowhere find,) order could have been preserved in an assembly of 600,000 men, their votes accurately numbered, and acts of violence prevented. If, however, we consider that, while Moses is said to have spoken to the whole congregation, he could not possibly be heard by 600,000 people, (for what human voice could be sufficiently strong to be so?) all our fears and difficulties will vanish; for this circumstance alone must convince any one that Moses could only have addressed himself to a certain number of persons deputed to represent the rest of the Israelites. Accordingly, in Numbers, 1:16, we find mention made of such persons. In contradiction to the common Israelites, they are there denominated Kerüe Häeda (קרואי העדה), that is, those wont to be called to the convention. In the 16th chapter of the same book, verse 2, they are styled Nesïe Eda Kerüe Moed

(נשיאי עדה קרואי מועד,) that is, chiefs of the community, that are called to the convention. I notice this passage particularly, because it appears from it that 250 persons of this description, who rose up against Moses, became to him objects of extreme terror; which they could not have been, if their voices had not been, at the same time, the voices of their families and tribes. Still more explicit, and to this point, is the passage Deut. 29 : 10, where Moses, in a speech to the whole people, says, 'Ye stand this day, all of you, before the Lord your God; your captains of your tribes, (that is, chiefs of tribes,) your elders and your officers, with all the men of Israel, your little ones, your wives, and thy stranger that is in thy camp, from the hewer of thy wood unto the drawer of thy water.' Now, as Moses could not possibly speak loud enough to be heard by two millions and a half of people, (for to so many did the Israelites amount, women and children included,) it must be manifest that the first-named persons represented the people, to whom they again repeated the words of Moses.

"Whether these representatives were on every occasion obliged to collect and declare the sense of their constituents, or whether, like the members of the English House of Commons, they acted in the plenitude of their own power for the general good, without taking instructions from their constituents, I find nowhere expressly determined; but methinks, from a perusal of the Bible, I can scarcely doubt that the latter was the case."

We presume few can have any doubt in the matter; and, as Jahn remarks in his Archæology, we do not find the people discovering any inclination to interfere in the deliberations of their representatives by dictating the course to be pursued. But, as he adds, important measures were often laid before the people for their consent or ratification; and this was done whenever the rulers or representatives thought it expedient to have the views of the whole nation so expressed.

NOTE E.—LECTURE 2, p. 65.

The account which I have given respecting the organization of the Courts of Justice, and the Confederation of the Tribes, is fully sustained by proofs which are stated with much detail by Michaelis in his Commentaries, and by Jahn in his Archœology. But while I refer to these authors as valuable expositors on these subjects, I cannot but differ from them with regard to the Council of Seventy, or the Sanhedrim, as it is often called. Jahn's views are very much taken from Michaelis', and I will quote only the words of the latter :—

"Moses established in the Wilderness another institution, which has been commonly held to be of a judicial nature; and, under the name of Sanhedrim or Synedrium, much spoken of both by Jews and Christians, although it probably was not of long continuance. We have the account of its establishment in Numbers, 11; and if we read the passage impartially and without prejudice, we shall probably entertain an opinion of the Synedrium different from that generally received, which exalt it into a supreme College of Justice that was to endure for ever.

"A rebellion that arose among the Israelites distressed Moses exceedingly. In order to alleviate the weight of the burden that oppressed him, he chose, from the twelve tribes collectively, a council of seventy persons, to assist him. These, however, could hardly have been judges; for, of them the people already had between sixty and seventy thousand. Besides, of what use could seventy new judges, or a Supreme Court of Appeal, have been in crushing a rebellion. It seems much more likely that this selection was intended for a Supreme Senate, to take a share with Moses in the Government: and as it consisted of persons of respectability, either in point of family or merit, it would serve materially to support his power and influence among the people in general. By a mixture of aristocracy, it would moderate the monarchical appearance which the constitution must have assumed, from Moses giving his laws by command of God: and it would unite a number of powerful families together, from their being all associated with Moses in the Government.

"It is commonly supposed that this Synedrium continued permanent; but this I doubt. For, in the whole period from the death of Moses to the Babylonish captivity, we find not the least mention of it in the Bible; and this silence, methinks, is decisive; for in the time of the judges, but particularly on those occasions when, according to the expression of the Book of Judges, 'There was neither king nor judge in Israel;' and again, during those great political revolutions, when David by degree became king over all the tribes, and when the ten tribes revolted from his grandson Rehoboam; and lastly, under the tyrannical reigns of some of the subsequent kings—such a supreme council of seventy persons, if it had been in existence, must have made a conspicuous figure in the history; and yet we find not the least trace of it; so that it merely appears to have been a temporary council, instituted by Moses for his personal service and security; and as he did not fill up the vacancies occasioned in it by deaths, it must have died out altogether in the Wilderness.

"No doubt the Jews, after their return from the Babylonish captivity, *did* institute a Sanhedrim at Jerusalem, of which frequent mention is made, not only in the New Testament, but also in Jewish writings. But this is merely an imitation of the ancient Mosaic Synedrium, with the nature of whose constitution the latter Jews were no longer acquainted; for they had indeed become ignorant of almost all the customs of their ancestors. The detail of this second Sanhedrim established by the latter Jews, belong not to our present work, but to their history after the Babylonish captivity."

In reference to the "ignorance of all the customs of their ancestors," which is here charged upon the Jews after the Captivity in Babylon, I remark that we should be very slow to believe such a charge against Ezra, Nehemiah, and others, under whose direction the restoration of the Jews and of their ordinances is described to us as having taken place. Such men well understood the "nature of the constitution of the Mosaic Synedrium," when, as Michaelis admits, they introduced what they considered "an imitation of it."

As to his main argument, to show that the Council of Seventy was a mere temporary arrangement—viz. that we find no mention of it from the time of Moses until the Babylonish Captivity; I do not admit the fact to be so; and even if it was so, I would not admit the inference which he draws from the supposed silence. We do not infer that circumcision was discontinued among the Hebrews for centuries after the days of Joshua because there is no express mention of its observance; nor that a Sabbath was not observed among the Patriarchs because the Scriptures are silent respecting it.

The Council, or Senate of Seventy, seems to be mentioned on just such occasions after the death of Moses as most fitly calls for it. It is of small consequence whether we may or may not find the name, if we find the thing. Our first inquiry, then, should be: What was this Council of Seventy? what were its rank, its authority, and duties? These, we may learn from the circumstances under which it was formed, and the occasion which gave rise to it, as we find them, Numbers, 11.

It has been observed (I believe by M'Intosh) that "institutions grow, and are not made." This is generally true; and the institution of the Seventy Elders seems to have grown out of the accumulation of business which arose from the increasing number and interests of the Hebrews on their way to Canaan.

An open rebellion had broken out among the people, in which they expressly avowed their desire to return to Egypt, and put designed contempt on the mercies which God had shown to them. The occurrence afflicted and displeased Moses exceedingly, and led him to ask for death rather than the continuance of a life which was harassed and burdened by the care of so wayward and ungrateful a people. He felt that notwithstanding the relief which he had gained from the appointment of rulers to aid him, as described, Deuteronomy, 1 : 9–18, yet there was an oppressive amount of care and responsibility still resting upon him. "Small matters" were decided by them; but every "great matter," every "hard cause," the people were still allowed to bring to him; and such were the constantly multiplying concerns of the people, that, as he here says, it had become too heavy for him to act "alone" as the highest authority for the judgment of "hard causes" or "great matters." He needed men for his aid to whom should be given "the Spirit" which had been given to him, a Spirit qualifying them to judge in matters which he alone had heretofore held under his jurisdiction. Accordingly he was told that the needful relief should be given: "The Lord said unto Moses, Gather unto you seventy men of the elders of Israel, whom thou knowest to be the elders of the people and officers over them, and bring them unto the tabernacle of the congregation, that they may stand there with thee. And I will come down and talk with thee there; and I will take of the Spirit which is upon thee, and will put it upon them, and they shall bear the burden of the people with thee, that thou bear it not thyself alone." Now, observe how these seventy are to be selected for this high office.

1. They were to be taken out of the Elders or Senators of Israel—must be men who had held the office and knew its duties. Elders or Senators, I say; for, as all scholars know, these terms are of similar import. Both of them originally refer to qualifications of age, but in time became terms of office, properly of such offices as could be best filled by men who had reached maturity of years.

2. They must have acquired acknowledged characteı and distinction among the elders—" Whom thou knowest to be elders." And then, besides this,

3. They must also have reputation as officers שׁטרים over the people. This is a title generally denoting preeminence or superior influence and authority, for whatever purpose the office was held. It is applied, for instance, to the commander-in-chief of an army.

4. They are described also, verse 26, as "those that were written;" implying that their names had been enrolled on a distinctive record, perhaps in this way to be submitted to some constituency for an election.

5. The number, seventy, of which the council was composed, is worthy of note. "Seven" and "seventy" are often called the sacred numbers, or numbers of perfection, in Scripture language; and with reference to this general idea, the Sanhedrim was made to consist of seventy, the more fully to denote its high rank.

Such were the origin, rank, and character of the Sanhedrim or Senate of Seventy, created by Divine appointment in the Hebrew Commonwealth. It seems, in some respects, to have been like an Upper House, as the Senate in our own Government; or, in other respects, like a High Court of Appeal, whose decisions and ordinances were final, and whose character for wisdom and integrity would give weight to their proceedings and their acts. So far from such a Senate being of no use in crushing a rebellion, as Michaelis intimates, its influence must have been most effective, not only in quelling rebellions that might arise, but in preventing those which might be threatened. Especially was it of use for this purpose at the time of its creation, when God gave his sanctions to its decisions by such a marked bestowment of His Spirit on its members as made itself obvious to all the people. Whether assembled at "the tabernacle of the congregation," or whether "remaining at the camp," we are told, "they prophesied and did not cease."

As to future mention of this distinguished or higher body of elders or senators, it may be found on several occasions in the history of the nation. In Joshua, 9: 13–21, when the treaty was made with the Gibeonites, which created much murmuring among the people, we find a body of men acting with Joshua as his council, who were called "Princes" or "Principal men of the Congregation," whose rank or authority evidently corresponded with that of the Senate or Council of Seventy, as described on the occasion of their original appointment. It is the same body of men who seem to have been referred to, Judges, 21: 16, under the title, "Elders of the Congregation," who gave their judgment on the great national question of preventing "a tribe from being destroyed out of Israel." It is not unlikely that this Senate was at times of defection from God, both "in the days of the Judges" and during the times of the Kings, allowed to fall into neglect. And if we look carefully at the reforms accomplished by Jehoshaphat, as described, Second Chronicles, 29 : 8–11, we may learn that one of his chief measures was the restoration of this very Council to its rightful place and authority. That Ezra acted with it and through it in his administration, seems to be admitted on all hands. It is to these Judges or Senators he is supposed to refer, Ezra, 10: 8.

NOTE F.—Lecture 2, p. 70.

A cursory perusal of the Book of Judges may have led some readers to a different conclusion, respecting the condition of the nation, while "the Judges ruled over Israel," from what I have described. The references, however, to this period of history which I have quoted from subsequent parts of the Bible, are decisive on the point. It should be remembered that this Book, short as it is, spreads over a period of about three hundred years; and, as a venerable commentator remarks, in a history so succinct, historians generally select the startling events of wickedness and violence, while they pass by in silence the more unobtrusive occurrences, which are the fruits of piety towards God and righteousness towards man. "And the land had rest fourscore years," is the brief language in which is described a period of unbroken peace and prosperity which lasted for nearly three generations, as we would term it. Besides, the crimes that stain these brief pages are exceeded by those which were committed after "the time of the Judges." Amidst the worst extremities of guilt and suffering to which reference is here made, there is nothing so atrocious and revolting as parents devouring their own children, or offering them in sacrifice to Moloch, which are recorded as sins committed during the reign of the Kings. It is true that during the reign of Solomon the nation acquired wealth, refinement, and distinction, never known till that day. But this arose chiefly from the unparalleled wisdom of the man who then wore the crown; and the disasters which followed Solomon's death soon showed how very unstable are the power and prosperity of a nation if it rests on the wisdom and virtue of any one man, rather than on the intelligence and integrity of the people themselves.

But whatever else may be left in uncertainty as to the comparative welfare of the people, under the two respective governments, one thing is certain—the union of the nation was preserved during the four hundred, or rather four hundred and fifty (see Acts, 13 : 20) years of the Republic; whereas, but one hundred and twenty years had passed under the government of the Kings, till the nation was rent in twain by a breach that never was healed, and which led to bloody and disastrous wars. It is also to be observed, that the greatest evils which transpired during the Commonwealth are described as springing from the want of a supreme Government over the entire nation. In connection with the disorders that resulted in the fatal war with the tribe of Benjamin, it is said: "In those days there was no King in Israel; every man did that which was right in his own eyes." Commentators, very much with one consent, interpret these words, not as referring to the want of a monarch with royal power and prerogatives, but to the want of that supreme authority over the whole people, which God had taught them how to provide and to perpetuate; which, after the days of Moses, is described as vested in Joshua and the Elders or Senators who were his contemporaries, and during whose administration Israel obeyed the Lord and "dwelt safely." That such is a just interpretation of the word "King," may be seen by referring to several passages, as Deut. 33 : 5, where Moses is said to have been "king in Jeshurun."

NOTE G. Lecture 2, p. 74.

This irrational and unscriptural doctrine, usually termed "the Divine right," may be said to have been first openly avowed under the sanction of James I, who had a strange faculty of giving the most offensive form to the most extravagant opinions, and who valued himself highly on his skill in kingcraft. It was not long before the University of Oxford threw all her weight in his favor; and to what length she carried her doctrines, may be seen from the following incident, to which others of a like character might be added by any one who is familiar with the events of that day.

"In 1662 the Rev. Mr. Knight, of Pembroke College, Oxford, delivered a sermon before the University, in which he contended that subordinate magistrates might lawfully use force against the chief magistrate in the following cases: 1. When the chief magistrate becomes a tyrant; 2. When he forces his subjects to blasphemy or idolatry; 3. When intolerable burdens or pressures are laid upon them; 4. When resistance is the only expedient to secure their lives, their fortunes, and the liberty of their consciences.

"Such heresy was not to be allowed. The preacher was sent for to court, and was required to give his authority for the doctrine above stated. He referred to the Commentary of Paræus on the thirteenth chapter of Romans, but relied upon King James himself as his chief authority, as the King was then assisting the oppressed inhabitants of Rochelle in opposing their Prince.

"The result of this reply was two-fold. The preacher was committed to prison, and Paræus' book was ordered to be burned at Oxford, Cambridge and London.

"The authorities of the University of Oxford then assembled, and condemned the preacher's assertions, and passed the following decree: 'That it is not lawful to resist the Sovereign, by force of arms, either offensively or defensively, *upon any pretence whatever;* that all doctors, masters of arts, &c., within the University, shall subscribe to these decrees and censures; and that whosoever takes any degree, shall take his oath, that he doth from his heart not only condemn the said doctrine of Paræus, but that he will neither preach, teach, nor maintain the same, or any of them, at any time in future.'"

Not long afterwards, a similar conflagration took place at Oxford. In the reign of Charles, and on the very day, as we are told, on which Russell was put to death, the University, by a public act, adopted in their fullest extent the doctrines of Filmer, and ordered the political works of Buchanan, Milton and Baxter to be burnt in the courts of the schools.

Mr. Knight is far from being the only English clergyman who has resisted and exposed these Oxford tenets. Dr. Paley has remarked, in his own terse style, that the Divine right of kings is like the Divine right of constables; neither of them having any right to authority, except so far as they are useful in maintaining government and good order. It is said, however, that the boldness and strength of Paley's reasoning on Civil Government, so far from being honored, was never forgiven by the dominant party of his day.

NOTE H.—Lecture 2, p. 75.

As this is a question which has been debated with much earnestness, and is now viewed with fresh interest, as it has a close application to the events of our day, I here quote the views of two very distinguished men, who contemplated the subject from different points of observation. The first is well known as a divine and a casuist, the other as a statesman and an historian.

President Dwight in his "Theology," having described the duty of subjects to their rulers, proceeds to say:

"The observations already made concerning this general subject, will prepare the way for settling our opinions concerning a particular question involved in it, which is of high importance to mankind. It is this: *Whether a nation is warranted to resist rulers, when seriously encroaching on its liberties?* It is my intention to confine the answer, which will now be given to this question, to *the lawfulness of such resistance. The expediency of it* I shall suppose to be granted, so far as the safety and success of the resistance is concerned. In other words, I shall suppose the people immediately interested in the question, to have as fair an opportunity as can be reasonably expected of preserving or acquiring political liberty, and of establishing, after the contest is ended, a free and happy government. In this case, the resistance in question is, in my own view, warranted by the Law of God. It is well known that this opinion has been adopted by some wise and good men, and denied by others. But the reasons alleged by both classes for their respective doctrines have, so far as they have fallen under my observation, been less satisfactory than I wished.

"A nation already free ought, whenever encroachments upon its freedom are begun, to reason in some such manner as the following:

"*Despotism, according to the universal and uniform experience of man, has regularly been fatal to every human interest.* It has attacked private happiness, and invaded public prosperity. It has multiplied sufferings without number and beyond degree. It has visited, regularly, the nation, the neighborhood, and the fireside, and carried with it public sorrow and private anguish. Personal liberty has withered at its touch; and national safety, peace, and prosperity have faded at its approach. Enjoyment has fled before it, life expired, and hope vanished. Evils of this magnitude have all been suffered, also, merely to gratify the caprice, the pride, the ambition, the avarice, the resentment, or the voluptuousness of one, or a few individuals; each of whose interests is of the same value in the sight of God, and no more than those of every other individual belonging to the nation. Can there be a reason—do the Scriptures furnish one?—why the millions of the present generation, and the numerous millions of succeeding generations, should suffer these evils merely to gratify the lusts of ten, twenty, or one hundred of their fellow men?

"If an affirmative answer should be given to this question, let it be remembered that *the same despotic power has, with equal regularity, cut off from subjects the means of usefulness and duty.* Mankind are sent into the world to serve God and do good to each other. If these things are not done, we live in vain, and worse than in vain. If the means of doing them are taken away, we are prevented, just so far, from answering the end of our creation. In vain is mental and bodily energy, in vain are talents, opportunities, and privileges bestowed by our Creator, if they are to be wrested from us by our fellow men, or the means of creating them taken away. In vain are we constituted parents, if we are precluded from procuring the comfortable sustenance, providing for the education, and promoting the piety and salvation of our offspring. In vain are we made children, if we are forbidden to perform the filial duties. In vain are we placed in other relations of life, if we are prohibited from performing the duties to which they give birth. Take away usefulness from man, and there is nothing left which is good, but everything which is bad. This good, however, despots have in a dreadful manner either prevented or destroyed. They have shrunk the talents, and palsied the energy of the mind—have shut the door of knowledge and blocked up the path of virtue—have wilted the human race into sloth and imbecility, and lowered the powers of man almost to the level of brutism. *The little spot of Greece* exhibited more energy and more specimens of mental greatness, in one hundred and fifty years, than the *Chinesian World* has exhibited in two thousand.

"But this is not all. *Despotic Rulers have exercised a most malignant influence upon the virtue of mankind.* They have assumed the prerogative of Heaven, and prescribed, as the will of God, a system of religious doctrines and duties to their subjects. This system has invariably been absurd, gross, and monstrous. The morality which it enjoins has been chiefly a code of crimes, fitter for the regulation of banditti than of sober men. The religion which it has taught has been a scheme of impiety. Yet this system they have enforced by the most terrible penalties—by the loss of property, liberty, and life—by the jail and the gibbet, the wheel and the rack, the faggot and the cross. Blood has stained the sceptre; martyrs have surrounded the throne.

"Even this is not all. *Despots, bad men themselves, must be served by bad men.* The baleful and deleterious influence of the head and members united, has extended everywhere, even to the corner and the cottage, and, like the deadly damp of the cavern, has imperceptibly and silently extinguished light and life wherever it has spread. Virtue has fallen amid the exhalation, unobserved and unknown. In its place has arisen and flourished a train of monstrous corruptions, which, with continually increasing strength, have finally gained entire possession of the land. Degenerated beyond recall, and polluted beyond hope, a people under this influence has sunk into remediless ruin, and only continued to exist until Mercy was wearied out by their profligacy, and reluctantly gave the sign for Vengeance to sweep them away. One regular and complete example of all these evils is given us by the voice of God himself in the kingdom of *Israel.* Profane history records a multitude. Is there any principle, either scriptural or natural, which demands of any nation such a sacrifice?

"But were we to admit that such a sacrifice might lawfully be made, *so far as ourselves only are concerned,* it is further to be remembered, that *we are entrusted with all the possessions, privileges, blessings, and hopes of our offspring, through every succeeding generation.* Guardians appointed by God himself, how can we fail of discharging punctiliously this sacred trust? The deposit is of value, literally immense. It involves the education, the comfort, the safety, the usefulness, the religious system, the morals, the piety, and the eternal life of millions, which can neither be known nor calculated. This is a trust which cannot lawfully be given up, unless in obedience to a known and unequivocal command of God; and no such command can be pleaded. Equally important is it that we prevent (for, under God, none but we can prevent) the contrary innumerable and immeasurable evils.

"At the same time, it is ever to be remembered that, under a free government, all the blessings which I have mentioned, so far as they are found in the present world, live and prosper, Such a government is the soil and the climate, the rain and the sunshine, of human good. Despotism, on the contrary, is the combined drought and sterility of *Nubia,* the frost and darkness of *Zembla,* amid which virtue, comfort, and safety can never spring.

"With these considerations in view, it is unquestionably evident to me that nations are bound, so far as it is possible, to maintain their freedom, and to resist every serious encroachment upon it, with such efforts as are necessary for its preservation."

Macaulay, in his recent "History of England," describes

the change which took place on this subject in the minds of many, when they saw how James II was overturning the civil and religious liberties of the realm:—

"The greatest Anglican doctors of that age had maintained that no breach of law or contract, no excess of cruelty, rapacity, or licentiousness, on the part of a rightful king, could justify his people in withstanding him by force. Some of them had delighted to exhibit the doctrine of non-resistance in a form so exaggerated as to shock common sense and humanity. They frequently and emphatically remarked, that Nero was at the head of the Roman Government when St. Paul inculcated the duty of obeying magistrates. The inference which they drew was, that if an English king should, without any law but his own pleasure, persecute his subjects for not worshipping idols—should fling them to the lions in the Tower—should wrap them up in pitched cloth, and set them on fire to light up St. James's Park—and should go on with these massacres till whole towns and shires were left without one inhabitant, the survivors would still be bound meekly to submit, and to be torn in pieces or roasted alive without a struggle. The arguments in favor of this proposition were futile indeed: but the place of sound argument was amply supplied by the omnipotent sophistry of interest and of passion."

Having remarked that "the system of Filmer might have survived the attacks of Locke, but never recovered the deadly blows given by James," he goes on to show how the truth now presented itself to those who formerly shut their eyes against it:—

"The ethical parts of Scripture were not to be construed like Acts of Parliament, or like the casuistical treatises of the schoolmen. What Christian really turned the left cheek to the ruffian who had smitten the right? What Christian really gave his cloak to the thieves who had taken his coat away? Both in the Old and the New Testaments, general rules were perpetually laid down unaccompanied by the exceptions. Thus there was a general command not to kill, unaccompanied by any reservation in favor of the warrior who kills in defence of his king and country. There was a general command not to swear, unaccompanied by any reservation in favor of the witness who swears to speak the truth before a judge. Yet the lawfulness of defensive war, and of judicial oaths, was disputed only by a few obscure sectaries, and was positively affirmed in the articles of the Church of England. All the arguments which showed that the Quaker, who refused to bear arms or to kiss the Gospels, was unreasonable and perverse, might be turned against those who denied to subjects the right of resisting tyranny by force. If it was contended that the texts which prohibited homicide, and the texts which prohibited swearing, though generally expressed, must be construed in subordination to the great commandment by which every man is enjoined to promote the welfare of his neighbors, and would, when so construed, be found not to apply to cases in which homicide or swearing might be absolutely necessary to protect the dearest interests of society, it was not easy to deny that the texts which prohibited resistance ought to be construed in the same manner. If the ancient people of God had been directed sometimes to destroy human life, and sometimes to bind themselves by oaths, they had also been directed sometimes to resist wicked princes. If early Fathers of the Church had occasionally used language which seemed to imply that they disapproved of all resistance, they had also occasionally used language which seemed to imply that they disapproved of all war and of all oaths. In truth, the doctrine of passive obedience, as taught at Oxford in the reign of Charles II, can be deduced from the Bible only by a mode of interpretation which would irresistibly lead us to the conclusions of Barclay and of Penn.

"It was not merely by arguments drawn from the letter of Scripture, that the Anglican theologians had, during the years which immediately followed the Restoration, labored to prove their favorite tenet. They had attempted to show that, even if Revelation had been silent, reason would have taught wise men the folly and wickedness of all resistance to established government. It was universally admitted that such resistance was, except in extreme cases, unjustifiable. And who would undertake to draw the line between extreme cases and ordinary cases? Was there any government in the world under which there were not to be found some discontented and factious men who would say, and perhaps think, that their grievances constituted an extreme case? If, indeed, it were possible to lay down a clear and accurate rule, which might forbid men to rebel against Trajan, and yet leave them at liberty to rebel against Caligula, such a rule might be highly beneficial. But no such rule had ever been, or ever would be, framed. To say that rebellion was lawful under some circumstances, without accurately defining those circumstances, was to say that every man might rebel whenever he thought fit; and a society in which every man rebelled whenever he thought fit, would be more miserable than a society governed by the most cruel and licentious despot. It was therefore necessary to maintain the great principle of non-resistance in all its integrity. Particular cases might doubtless be put in which resistance would benefit a community; but it was, on the whole, better that the people should patiently endure a bad government, than that they should relieve themselves by violating a law on which the security of all government depended.

"Such reasoning easily convinced a dominant and prosperous party, but could ill bear the scrutiny of minds strongly excited by royal injustice and ingratitude. It is true that, to trace the exact boundary between rightful and wrongful resistance, is impossible; but this impossibility arises from the nature of right and wrong, and is found in almost every part of ethical science. A good action is not distinguished from a bad action by marks so plain as those which distinguish a hexagon from a square. There is a frontier where virtue and vice fade into each other. Who has ever been able to define the exact boundary between courage and rashness, between prudence and cowardice, between frugality and avarice, between liberality and prodigality? Who has ever been able to say how far mercy to offenders ought to be carried, and where it ceases to deserve the name of mercy and becomes a pernicious weakness? What casuist, what lawgiver, has ever been able nicely to mark the limits of the right of self-defence? All our jurists hold that a certain quantity of risk to life or limb justifies a man in shooting or stabbing an assailant; but they have long given up, in despair, the attempt to describe, in precise words, that quantity of risk. They only say that it must be, not a slight risk, but a risk such as would cause serious apprehension to a man of firm mind; and who will undertake to say what is the precise amount of apprehension which deserves to be called serious, or what is the precise texture of mind which deserves to be called firm? It is doubtless to be regretted that the nature of words and the nature of things do not admit of more accurate legislation;

nor can it be denied that wrong will often be done when men are judges in their own cause, and proceed instantly to execute their own judgment. Yet who would, on that account, interdict all self-defence? The right which a people has to resist a bad government bears a close analogy to the right which an individual, in the absence of legal protection, has to slay an assailant. In both cases the evil must be grave. In both cases all regular and peaceable modes of defence must be exhausted before the aggrieved party resorts to extremities. In both cases an awful responsibility is incurred. In both cases the burden of the proof lies on him who has ventured on so desperate an expedient; and, if he fails to vindicate himself, he is justly liable to the severest penalties. But in neither case can we absolutely deny the existence of the right. A man beset by assassins is not bound to let himself be tortured and butchered without using his weapons because nobody has ever been able precisely to define the amount of danger which justifies homicide. Nor is a society bound to endure passively all that tyranny can inflict because nobody has ever been able precisely to define the amount of misgovernment which justifies rebellion.

"But could the resistance of Englishmen to such a prince as James be properly called rebellion? The thorough-paced disciples of Filmer, indeed, maintained that there was no difference whatever between the polity of our country and that of Turkey; and that, if the King did not confiscate the contents of all the tills in Lombard-street, and send mutes with bow-strings to Sancroft and Halifax, this was only because his Majesty was too gracious to use the whole power which he derived from Heaven. But the great body of Tories—though, in the heat of conflict, they might occasionally use language which seemed to indicate that they approved of these extravagant doctrines—heartily abhorred despotism. The English Government was, in their view, a limited monarchy. Yet how can a monarchy be said to be limited if force is never to be employed, even in the last resort, for the purpose of maintaining the limitations? In Muscovy, where the sovereign was, by the constitution of the state, absolute, it might perhaps be with some color of truth contended that, whatever excesses he might commit, he was still entitled to demand, on Christian principles, the obedience of his subjects. But here prince and people were alike bound by the laws. It was therefore James who incurred the woe denounced against those who insult the powers that be. It was James who was resisting the ordinance of God, who was mutinying against that legitimate authority to which he ought to have been subject, not only for wrath, but also for conscience sake, and who was, in the true sense of the words of Jesus, withholding from Cæsar the things which were Cæsar's."

NOTE I.—Lecture 2, p. 82.

Although Michaelis at first rather denies what in the end he seems to admit as the great moral duty enforced in this command, yet as his remarks contain several curious and interesting facts, I have made the following extracts from them:—

"It is the command of Moses, that if a person find a bird's nest in the way, whether on a tree or on the ground, though he may take the eggs or the young, he shall not take the mother, but always allow her to escape. It is clear that he here speaks, not of those birds which nestle upon people's property—in other words, that he does not, for instance, prohibit an Israelite from totally destroying a sparrow's or a swallow's nest that might happen to be troublesome to him, or to extirpate, to the utmost of his power, the birds that infested his field or vineyard. He merely enjoins what one was to do on finding such nests *on the way*—that is, *without* one's property; thus guarding against the utter extinction, or too great diminution, of any species of bird indigenous to the country. And this, in some countries, is still, with respect to partridges, an established rule; which, without a special law, is observed by every real sportsman, and the breach of which subjects him to the reproaches of his brethren."

It is a singular fancy in Michaelis, that he should interpret the words, "in the way," to mean, "without one's property." Birds have no partiality for building their nests on the public road or on the wayside. On the contrary, they seek retirement, and build their nests where secrecy gives them most security from discovery and violation. When

Moses speaks of a "bird's nest that may chance to be before us in the way," he refers to a nest that a man might find in his way wherever he might chance to be going, whether in the fields or in the woods. Besides, as Moses is here speaking of birds and fowls generally, why should a man be told to take only the eggs or young, which may be valuable for food, if found on the wayside, implying that he must not touch them if found on his own premises? Or, if we suppose Moses to be here speaking of birds that may be an injury to the fields if greatly multiplied, why is he so careful to teach that the young or the eggs must be destroyed, if found without a man's premises, making no reference to those found within his enclosures? Such birds especially, have no great regard for the landmarks which define property.—Michaelis proceeds:

"Nor would any further illustration be necessary if Moses spoke only of edible birds, and as if merely concerned for their preservation. But this is not the case. His expression is so general, that we must needs understand it of all birds whatever, even those that are most destructive, besides what are properly birds of prey. And here many readers may think it strange, that Moses should be represented as providing for the preservation of noxious birds; yet, in fact, nothing can be more conformable to legislative wisdom, especially on the introduction of colonies into a new country. To extirpate, or even to persecute to too great an extent, any species of birds in such a country, from an idea, often too hastily entertained, of its being hostile to the interests of the inhabitants, is a measure of very doubtful policy. It ought, in general, to be considered as a part of Nature's bounty, bestowed for some important purpose; but what that is, we certainly discover too late, when it has been extirpated, and the evil consequences of that measure are begun to be felt.

"In this matter the legislator should take a lesson from the naturalist. Linnæus, whom all will allow to be a perfect master in the science of Natural History, has made the above remark in his dissertation, entitled 'Historia Naturalis cui Bono?' and gives two remarkable examples to confirm it; the one in the case of the *Little Crow of Virginia*, extirpated at great expense on account of its supposed destructive effects, and which the inhabitants would soon gladly have re-introduced at double expense. The account of the circumstance is given in the 'Hanover Magazine' for the year 1767, as follows:—'In the English colonies of North America, it was remarked that a certain sort of crow frequented the peas fields; and in order to put a stop to its ravages for ever, its utter extirpation was resolved on. But this was no sooner effected, than an insect of the beetle kind, which had always been known also to do some mischief to the peas, multiplied to such a degree that very few peas were left. An intelligent naturalist thought this occurrence worth investigation, and found that the crows were not in quest of peas, but only devouring these beetles; and, of course, that had they not been extirpated, these insects could not have increased so much, and the crops of peas would have been more abundant. At somewhat less expense the same truth was, some time ago, confirmed in Sweden. The common crow was thought to be too fond of the young roots of grass, being observed sometimes to pick them out and lay them bare. Orders were therefore given to the people to be at all pains to extirpate them, till some person, more judicious, opposed this, and showed that it was not the roots of the grass, but the destructive caterpillars of certain insects which fed on them, that the crows searched for and devoured.' Every one knows what vexation sparrows occasion to the owners of gardens and corn fields. In the year 1745 fields were not unfrequently to be seen so completely destroyed, that scarcely the seed remained; and in the gardens which they haunt, they pick the peas, when they spring out of the earth, with such avidity that a crop cannot be raised. Their excessive multiplication, therefore, ought certainly to be prevented; and it is the right and interest of every householder to extirpate them on his property. As the mischief they did, about thirty years ago, was so very great, particularly in Prussia, where the laws take more concern in matters of economy than in other countries, there took place, if I rightly remember, at the instigation of a person whose name was *Kretschmar*, such a violent persecution of the sparrows in Prussia, as if their utter extirpation had been determined on. This persecution was just, but it was carried too far, for *Kretschmar* was too great an enemy to the sparrows; being, indeed, a good economist, as far as a good head, without study, could make him so, but then quite unacquainted with Natural History. And the effects of his ignorance soon appeared; for caterpillars multiplied to such a pitch, that it was found necessary to put a stop to the persecution, that the sparrows might destroy them.

"It is quite a well-known circumstance, that in the year 1761, after the conclusion of the war, when the sparrows in this corner withdrew far from the city into the fields, because among the great quantity of spilled corn they found superabundance of food, it was impossible to protect the gardens about Gottingen from the depredations of the caterpillar.

"In North America another evil has been found to result from destroying too many of these birds. The gnats increased to such a degree, especially in moist places, that the people and cattle were harassed by them much more than formerly. These examples serve pretty strongly to show, that in respect at least to birds, we ought to place as much confidence in the wisdom and kindness of Nature, as not rashly to extirpate any species which she has established in a country as a great and perhaps indispensable blessing.

"That Moses should have affixed no punishment to the violation of this *game law*, (for such, in my opinion, is its most proper name,) but merely promised, and *that* almost in the language of the fifth commandment, blessings from heaven to those who observed it, for their compassion to animals and the mothers of animals, will not appear strange to any man that has any ideas of legislative policy. The blessing of God to the keepers of a law so important to Palestine, Moses certainly could promise with much more propriety than any of our legislators, because he spoke as a prophet, and as a legislator sent from God, and because the Israelitish Government had the form of a theocracy. But to none other, than a divinely-inspired legislator, is it competent to denounce curses, or promise blessings, in the name of the Most High.

"It is singular, after all, that the very blessing of the fifth commandment is annexed to this law. In following out the idea, we are almost tempted to believe that Moses had designed to connect this law for the preservation of birds, with that commandment; and to represent the mothers even of beasts as objects (of our veneration, shall I say? No, that were too much, but) of our dutiful regards; so that parents, even those of inferior animals, deserve to be viewed with emotions of tenderness and gratitude, in recompense, as it were, for their care in the propagation of their species."

These facts in natural history serve to show how little we understand of the wisdom and mercy with which the Most High has adapted one part of creation to meet the wants or condition of another. The wisest of men have yet much to learn on this subject. "O! Lord," says David, "how manifold are thy works; in wisdom hast thou made them all; the earth is full of thy riches." Every thing in the multiplied and manifold works of God is made to answer some purpose of perfect wisdom and rich goodness; and man in his ignorance often complains of that very thing as a tormenting evil, which is in reality an indispensable good.

NOTE K.—Lecture 3, p. 112.

Just after the delivery of these Lectures the treaty was made with Mexico, ceding to us New Mexico and California. Though this accession of territory may be said in one sense to have been gained by conquest, yet it results in the voluntary and anxious application of the people for admission into the Union. Our victory is far from reducing them to the condition of Colonies. It exalts them to an equality with ourselves in privileges, which they were desirous to enjoy; and severs them from a political connection which they had previously, and for years, been desirous to break.

This cession forms another link in the chain of events which men, "having knowledge of the times," have foretold during the last fifty years. It has now become the general opinion of those who study and understand the progress of nations, that the territory of the United States will ultimately embrace the whole of North America. The spirit of expansion and colonization which distinguish the Anglo-Saxon race, will necessarily either crowd off, or incorporate with themselves, the more indolent and effete races that now occupy regions capable of being turned to much better account, if in better hands. It should be our constant care that nothing be done for this object which would be a violation of our honor and regard for justice as a Christian nation. Events aré ripening spontaneously to give us increased territory quite as rapidly as we are ready to receive it, and to give it homogeneousness of character and spirit with our institutions. In former enlargements of the national boundaries the policy of the government has been eminently just and pacific. Louisiana became ours by purchase; Florida by friendly negociation with the parent State; and Texas by voluntary annexation. The origin of the war with Mexico involves questions on which it is nòt my province to pronounce; but it has led in the end, as all admit, to the payment of just debts long due to our citizens, and to the discovery of mineral wealth which will soon effect a great revolution in the commerce of the world, and which might have remained hidden and untouched for centuries had the country containing it, remained under its former rulers.

How soon other applications for incorporation into the Union may reach us, and whether they are to come from the North or the South, or simultaneously from both, time will show. But the public mind should become familiarized with the subject, for every intelligent observer of passing events must perceive that before long the nation will be called to act on the question.

NOTE L.—Lecture 3, p. 124.

The great difficulty of conveying Christian truth in Pagan languages has been felt by Missionaries in all Pagan countries. But the peculiarities of the Chinese spoken language enhance the difficulty to an extent that is but little understood. The subject is happily and briefly illustrated in the following extracts taken from the Fortieth Annual Report of the American Board of Commission for Foreign Missions. Speaking of China, they say,—

"In the opinion of the missionaries here, their future success in preaching will depend very much on their success in acquiring the *tones* and aspirates of the Chinese language, to which they are giving earnest attention. The written language may be understood without a knowledge of the tones; but in speaking, a correct use of them is indispensable. Without it, the speaker will be intelligible only to those who, being well acquainted with him, or with other unlearned foreigners like him, understand his ignorance, and can mentally correct his blunders as he proceeds.

"It is difficult to make this subject plain to the English reader. In our own language, the verb *lead*, and the noun *lead*, are written alike, but each has a different pronunciation and meaning from the other. Here, however, the vowel sounds in the two words are different. But in the Chinese spoken language, many words, having the same consonant and vowel sounds, and represented by the same written character, yet differing in signification, are distinguished by some peculiarity in the mode of pronunciation. These different spoken words, however, are usually spoken as the same word under different tones. Perhaps the word *there* affords the best illustration in our language. In the phrase, "and there died of the people seventy thousand men," it is a mere expletive without any distinct meaning. In the phrase, "and David built there an altar," it is an adverb of place. If it should be uttered in the first of these examples as in the last, it would change the meaning from a mere statement of the number that died, into an assertion that so many died in some specified place. On strict examination, probably, something of the same principle might be detected in most languages, but in no others is it known to be so important as in the Chinese. In the dialect spoken at Fuh-Chan, in many cases, the same written word may represent eight or ten spoken words, differing from each other in tone, aspiration, and meaning. Nor is it yet found that the ten or less different tones of the same written word have any natural or logical relation to each other. For example, the same Chinese character, the consonant and vowel sounds of which are represented by the same Roman letters, *pang*, represents ten distinct words in the spoken language, differing in tone and aspiration, and signifying, 1, to help; 2, a bee; 3, to bind; 4, to spin; 5, to let go; 6, corpulent; 7, a room; 8, a sail; 9, a club; 10, a seam. And yet these ten spoken words are readily distinguished by the Chinese ear; and whoever utters the written word *pang*, must of necessity utter it in some one of these ten ways, so as to express some one of these ideas to the exclusion of the rest."

NOTE M.—Lecture 4, p. 152.

I am aware that efforts have been made to discredit these tables of moral statistics. But facts and figures are stubborn things. Although the conclusions from the statements may have been carried somewhat too far, as is generally the case in all new modes of reasoning, they will be found substantially correct. Many of the tables have been prepared with indefatigable industry and great caution; and although the conclusions to which they lead tell with singular power in favor of Christianity as essential to the welfare of a people generally educated, the facts and figures leading to the conclusion were generally prepared by men who cannot be suspected of any partiality either for Christianity or the Bible which reveals it. Indeed, they admit in some cases that their investigations led to results which they were reluctant to embrace. M. d'Angeville, in his

Essay on the Moral and Intellectual Statistics of France, expressly declares that his mind had long combatted the evidence of facts on this subject, before his own investigations forced him to the conclusion that in France crime generally keeps pace with primary education.

The complicated action and reaction of various causes on the social and moral condition of a people should teach us to be cautious in the adoption of any specific theory. But there are some general conclusions so supported by an array of evidence that they cannot be denied. Readers who have not time to examine different authors on the subject, will find the whole question respecting the value of statistical information on crime and its causes happily presented in the *Edinburgh Review*, vol. 69, p. 47–74, where d'Angeville's work is reviewed, and such reference made to Quételet and others as may enable the reader to become acquainted with the more important features belonging to the question.

NOTE N.—Lecture 4, p. 159.

There are several judicial decisions which might be quoted on this subject, but I shall confine myself to a case recently decided by the Court of Errors in the State of South Carolina. It was that of a man who was prosecuted by the City Council of Charleston for selling goods on the Lord's day, or the Christian Sabbath. The decision was given against him, and in pronouncing the judgment of the Court, Judge O'Neall held the following language:—

"Crimes are classed into *Mala in se* and *Mala prohibita*. What gives them that character? We cannot answer, as the

Israelites would do, by pointing to Mount Sinai, and say the Lord God commanded us, saying, 'thou shalt not kill,' 'thou shalt not steal.' The authority of these divine precepts comes to us through Christianity. We are 'the wild olive tree grafted,' in place of the broken branches of the original tree, Israel. And hence the law delivered at Mount Sinai may be by us appealed to, as pointing out that which is '*evil in itself.*'

"Again, our law declares all contracts *contra bonos mores* as illegal and void. What constitutes the standard of good morals? Is it not Christianity? There certainly is none other. Say *that* cannot be appealed to, and I don't know what would be good morals. The day of moral virtue in which we live, would in an instant, if that standard were abolished, lapse into the dark and murky night of Pagan immorality. In this State the marriage tie is indissoluble. Whence do we take that maxim? It is from the teaching of the New Testament *alone.*

"In the courts over which we preside, we daily acknowledge Christianity as the most solemn part of our administration. A Christian witness, having no religious scruples against placing his hand upon the book, is sworn upon the holy Evangelists, the books of the New Testament, which testify of our Saviour's birth, life, death and resurrection. This is so common a matter, that it is little thought of as affording any evidence of the part which Christianity has in the common law.

"All blasphemous publications, carrying upon their face that irreverent rejection of God and his holy religion, which makes them dangerous to the community, have always been held to be libels, and punishable at common law. *Here* they would also be plain acts of licentiousness, having no warrant of protection whatever in our constitution. This, however, never could extend to free and manly discussion on these holy subjects. For I agree with Mr. Jefferson, (Notes on Va. 235,) 'Our rulers can have authority over such natural rights only as we have submitted to them. The rights of conscience we never submitted, we never could submit. We are answerable for them to our God!' But I should hesitate long in pushing the argument as far as he does by saying, as he does, that in its exercise 'it does me no injury for my neighbor to say there are twenty Gods, or no God.' While the argument rests only in words, it would be so evanescent that it might be no injury. But when it comes to be put in print

11*

to be read, like Paine's Age of Reason, by the young and the unwary, where is the parent who would say '*It does me no injury.*' I agree fully to what is beautifully and appropriately said in *Updegraff* v. *Commonwealth* (11 Serg. and Rawle, 394); 'Christianity, general Christianity, is, and always has been, part of the common law;' not Christianity founded on any particular religious tenets; not Christianity with an established church, and tithes, and spiritual courts· but Christianity with liberty of conscience to all men.

"But I nave said all which need be said on this interesting subject. It was not necessary for the decision of this case; it has only been said to prevent silence from being interpreted into a want of confidence in the proposition, that Christianity may be justly appealed to as part of our common law."

NOTE O.—Lecture 5, p. 170.

The oppression and gross inequalities of condition which have arisen from the possession of vast landed estates, are still very glaring in several of the nations in Europe. In Russia, for instance, the land is so entirely in the hands of the nobles as to keep the mass of the people in the most degrading slavery; and even in England, as may be seen from the following statement, much as she has done, and is doing, on behalf of her people, the immense estates held by the aristocracy are an insuperable bar against a general elevation of their condition. In a digest of Colman's recent work on Europe, published in several papers, it appears that

"Althorpe, the residence of Earl Spencer, consists of 10,000 acres, 'all lying together in wood, meadow, pasture, gardens, parks, and every thing in a style of superior beauty and order.' His house contains sleeping rooms for seventy guests—the entries and rooms are filled with pictures and statues. A gallery of pictures, one hundred feet long, contains many of the works of the first masters. His library comprises more than 50,000 volumes, and is said to be the finest private library in the world.

"The Duke of Richmond's home farm (Goodwood) consists of 23,000 acres. His whole domain at Goodwood is 40,000 acres. He has a summer retreat in Scotland of between 200,000 and 300,000 acres. 'Of the beauty and magnificence of this establishment,' says Mr. Colman, 'I cannot give you any adequate idea; —extensive parks through which you ride for miles and miles—herds of deer, sheep, and cattle. The Duke has more than forty race horses, and sixty grooms and hostlers. His salmon fisheries at the Gordon Castle used to be let for £10,000, and now lets for £7,000 per annum, or $35,000.

"The annual income of the Duke of Devonshire, the proprietor of Chatsworth, is said to be £200,000, or one million of dollars. This is said to be the most splendid nobleman's seat in the kingdom. His *arboretum*, covering many acres, contains one or more specimens of every tree that can be acclimated; the kitchen garden covers twelve acres; a conservatory, 387 feet long, 117 wide, 67 high, with a carriage-way. This conservatory is covered with 7,600 square feet of glass, and warmed with hot water, passing through an extent of seven miles. The fountain at Chatsworth throws the water to an height of 276 feet.

"Mr. Colman gives an account of several noblemen whose annual income varied from £100,000 to £150,000; that is, from $500,000 to $750,000. Speaking of Lord Yarborough, he says that his Lordship 'has an indefinite number of hunters, &c.' and adds—'It was the custom at this place for his Lordship, (and his guests were always invited to accompany him,) at nine o'clock precisely, in the evening, to visit the stables where the hunting and riding horses were kept, which were reached by a covered passage way from the house. The stables presented all the neatness of a house parlor, and the grooms were more than a dozen in number, all drawn up in a line to receive the company.' Lord Yarborough has more than 60,000 acres in his plantation; he has 600 tenants, and you can ride thirty miles in a direct line upon his estate. 'Many of the tenants of Lord Yarborough pay 1,000 and 1,400 guineas a year rent, and several of them live like noblemen, keeping their dogs, horses, carriages, and servants in livery.'

"After alluding to a court ball, at which one lady wore £60,000 or $300,000 worth of diamonds, Mr. C. remarks—'The Duchess of Roxburgh, whom I do not know, appeared most splendidly; and well she might, as the annual income of the Duke is stated to be £300,000.'"

We might add several others to the vast estates which he has enumerated. The property of the Dukes of Gordon, for instance, in the counties of Banff, Moray, Aberdeen, and Inverness, covers 422,000 acres; and if to this we add their estates on the Dee, their whole possessions will exceed 550,000 acres. The large estates in land held by proprietors in Ireland are a great obstacle in the way of the noble efforts which are made to elevate and improve the condition of the over-stocked population in that island. We cannot too highly commend, the efforts now made to remedy the evil, and to put the waste lands under cultivation by men who will have permanent interest in the soil.

NOTE P.—Lecture 5, 178.

Since the foregoing pages were in type, the Legislature of the State of New-York has passed a law for the exemption of the Homestead.

There were some exceptions to the law restoring the landed inheritance on the year of Jubilee, but not such as to impair its general effect; while to prevent the exceptions from being carried too far, they were defined with great care. In Lev. 27 : 16–21, it is enacted, that in case a man had consecrated a field to God, he might redeem it on paying the value of the crops till the coming Jubilee, and one fifth more to the priests. Otherwise, at the Jubilee, the field, instead of reverting to its former owner, became a part of the inheritance of the priesthood, as a thing devoted to the Lord.

There is an interpretation often given to the law in Deut. 15 : 1–11, which in this connection is deserving of attention. The enactment is considered by some as cancelling all debts due from one Hebrew to another every seventh year. Others consider the privilege ensured to the debtor every seventh year, as merely "a release" from a claim for payment on that year, in consequence of allowing his land to lie fallow, as the law required. Michaelis, in his commentary on this law, says:

"One privilege only did Moses concede to the debtors, and among a nation of husbandmen it was, indeed, an indispensable one. In the seventh year, during which all the land lay fallow, no debt could be exacted from a poor man, because then he had no income whence to pay it. To debtors not poor, this privilege did not apply; for the words immediately following in ver. 4 are, *save when he is not one of the poor among you, &c.* on which words others have put this strange construction, as if Moses, in a law enacted in favor of the poor, had promised there should be *no* poor among the Israelites; but they thus get into an embarrassment, in comparing one passage with another; since, in ver. 11 of this very chapter, he says, that there should *always* be poor persons among the Israelites. This law, besides, applied only to the Israelites, and not to strangers who possessed no land, and of course were not in the seventh year differently circumstanced, from what they were during the other six. Them, therefore, creditors might then sue for the payment of debt, with all rigor."

How far and how often the government of a country should interfere or enact laws for the release of debtors, has long been viewed as a very doubtful and difficult question of political economy. It has repeatedly occupied the attention of statesmen in our own nation, and much diversity of opinion respecting it prevails to this day. I will therefore make some further extracts from Michaelis, showing how a man of his mind and learning viewed the subject. In his commentary on the law above quoted, he adds:

"Many have been inclined so to understand this law, as if, in the seventh year, *all* debts were to be cancelled; and the Talmud has actually adopted this explanation, endeavoring withal to guard against the evils of the year of release, by all manner of moral considerations.

* * * * * * * * * * *

"That every seventh year all debts should be extinguished, is a law so absurd, so unjust, and so destructive to the interests of all classes of the community, that we are not warranted to ascribe it to a legislator, nor even to a turbulent tribune of the people, unless he has enacted it in terms the most express, and such as leave not the shadow of a doubt as to his meaning.

"There may, I grant, extraordinary cases occur, which render the extinction of all debts necessary; particularly when, by the charge of immoderate and usurious interest, or by any other artifices of moneyed men, they have become so enormous as that the state can no longer subsist under them. Thus among the Romans, *Novæ Tabulæ* were sometimes projected; a measure, however, which, by reason of the great confusion which it must have made in the commonwealth, was dreaded by every good citizen, and even by those that were themselves debtors, as a very great evil. I will farther admit, and therefore, I am here sufficiently liberal, that it may be a problem in politics, whether it might not be expedient that all debts should be extinguished every fifty or a hundred years; in order to avoid law-suits, which extend to so long a period, to secure property more effectually, and to prevent children and grandchildren from groaning under the heavy burdens of the debts of their forefathers? Such a periodical extinction of debts, in regard to which, however, to make it just, we must presuppose an expeditious administration of justice, in order to bring law-suits to an end before the year of remission, would have a strong resemblance to legal prescription; nor should I have had anything to object to it, if Moses (and thus Josephus explains him) had ordained the extinction of debts only every fiftieth year. But a septennial extinction of debts with *Novæ Tabulæ*, (a phrase which made the Roman state to tremble, when a tribune of the people but uttered it,) how great would be its injustice, and the misery it would occasion! Under such a law, none would be so foolish as to lend; so that those who stood in need of loans would only be in a worse predicament, through the mistaken clemency of the legislator. But what, above all, would be the absurdity of the exhortation in ver. 9, 10, *to lend to the poor, and not to entertain the base thought of the near approach of the seventh year; but however near it were, to let him have whatever he wanted,* were all debts cancelled every seventh year? Neither property nor honor could be secure, were such an exhortation respected. The poor might then, in the sixth year, impose the greatest hardships on the rich, and borrow from them to any extent, without repaying a farthing.

* * * * * * * * * * *

"Of the injustice of such a law, I shall say nothing; for of that every one will be sensible, who places himself in the situation of a person aware that to-morrow all debts become legally cancelled, to whom comes a poor man to-day, not asking an alms at the good pleasure of the giver, but demanding a loan determined in its magnitude by himself, and which, he is reminded, the law enjoins him not to be so hard-hearted and selfish as to refuse. I only ask this question: What country could subsist under such a law? Who could have any inclination to industry, or the acquisition of riches, if every seventh year his earnings lay at the mercy of every beggar? A country where laws so unjust prevailed, every man of wealth would be either compelled to leave, (and the sooner he did so the better;) or else, as is necessary under tyrannical governments, where the greedy despot seeks to lay hold of the property of his subjects, under every possible pretext, he must affect poverty, and live like a beggar. In either case, the poor, who most generally derive their subsistence from the rich, will be placed in circumstanstances truly deplorable.

"Has Moses, then, by the tenor of any of his other laws, deserved to have the reproach of such an absurdity cast upon him? By no means, in my judgment; and therefore it would be but fair to put upon his law concerning the seventh year, not an irrational, but a rational construction. The word *Schemitta* (שמטה

employed by Moses, and which Luther renders *Erloss*, (Eng. vers. *release*,) is, like many other terms of law, not so etymologically clear as could be wished. At the same time it includes nothing that indicates a total remission of debt. By a comparison with the Syriac and Arabic languages, its original signification would appear to have been, *suspend or let fall*.—The complete phrase, ver. 2, 3, means, *the creditor shall not in the seventh year let fall his hand* (Shamot Jado), which is equivalent to saying, he shall not seize the debtor, or as a Roman would have expressed it, *manum non injiciet:* and if there should be any doubt how Moses wished this to be understood, he himself explained it in ver. 2, by saying, *he shall not exact it of his debtor*. Here follow the words as I translate them, to a person who prefers having them, though in bad German, yet more close to the Hebrew: *Nach Ablauf von sieben Jahren sollst du* Schemitta *machen.* Schemitta *aber est, dass jeder Glaubijer der seinem Nachsten geborget hat, seine hand fallen lasst; er soll seinem Nachsten und Bruder nicht exequiren.* In English: After the expiration of seven years, thou shalt make a *Schemitta*; but a *Schemitta* is, that every creditor who has lent to his neighbor, let fall his hand; he shall not have recourse to legal execution on his neighbor and brother. Now, let every man judge for himself, which of these two things Moses intended—whether,

"1. In the seventh year, no debtors should be dunned, or debts sued for; which was a very rational precept, because then the Israelite derived no income from his land—or whether,

"2. In the seventh year all debts were to be completely and for ever extinguished, and without the creditor having it in his power to demand them either in the seventh or eighth or any subsequent year;—a precept which has not the most remote rational connexion with the *fallow* of the seventh year, but would have been altogether arbitrary and insulated."

NOTE Q.—Lecture 5, p. 208.

As an illustration of the success with which conflicting views have been reconciled in former times, I will refer to an incident in the history of the Convention which framed the Constitution of the United States; and I do it the more readily as the occasion formed an important crisis in the history of the nation, and we sometimes have accounts of the proceedings which do not accord with the facts. A correspondent of the *New-York Observer* has recently given the following spirited description of the whole scene:

"MESSRS. EDITORS,—The following narrative, relating a fine, not to say a sublime scene, in the Convention that framed the Constitution of the United States, was originally derived from Gen. Jonathan Dayton of Jersey. He was the '*Junior member*' that moved the '*re-consideration*' mentioned below. The account is full of interest and instruction at the present time, when the spirit of discord and selfishness is so rife in our national councils. *Would that a copy of it could be sent to every member of our National Legislature, and that it could be read by every Christian and patriot throughout the land.*

"I was (said General Dayton) a delegate from New Jersey in the General Convention which assembled in Philadelphia, for the purpose of digesting a Constitution for the United States, and I believe I was the youngest member of that body. The great and good Washington was then our President, and Dr. Franklin, among other great men, was a delegate from Pennsylvania. A disposition was soon discovered in some members to display themselves in oratorical flourishes—but the good sense and discretion of the majority put down all such attempts. We had convened to deliberate upon, and if possible effect, a great national object—to search for political wisdom and truth; these, we meant to pursue with simplicity, and to avoid every thing which would have a tendency to divert our attention or perplex our scheme.

"A great variety of projects were proposed—all republican in general outlines, but differing in their details. It was therefore determined that certain elementary principles should at the first be established in each branch of the intended Constitution,—and afterwards the details should be debated and filled up.

"There was little or no difficulty in determining upon the elementary principles—such as, for instance, that the government should be a republican representative government—that it should be divided into three branches, i. e. Legislative, Executive and

Judical, &c. But when the organization of the Legislative branch came under consideration, it was easy to be perceived that the Eastern and Southern States had distinct interests, which it was difficult to reconcile,—and that the larger States were disposed to form a constitution in which the smaller States would be mere appendages and satellites to the larger ones. On the first of these subjects much animated and somewhat angry debate had taken place, when the ratio of representation in the lower house of Congress was before us—the Southern States claiming for themselves the whole number of black population; while the Eastern States were for confining the elective franchise to freemen only, without respect to color.

"As the different parties adhered pertinaciously to their different positions, it was feared that this would prove an insurmountable obstacle; but as the members were already generally satisfied that no constitution could be formed, which would meet the views and subserve the interests of each individual State, it was evident that it must be a matter of compromise and mutual concession. Under these impressions, and with these views, it was agreed at length that each State should be entitled to one delegate in the House of Representatives for every 30,000 of its inhabitants—in which number should be included three-fifths of the whole number of their slaves.

"When the details of the House of Representatives were disposed of, a more knotty point presented itself in the organization of the Senate. The larger States contended that the same ratio as to States should be common to both branches of the Legislature; or, in other words, that each State should be entitled to a representation in the Senate, (whatever might be the number fixed on,) in proportion to its population, as in the House of Representatives. The smaller States on the other hand contended, that the House of Representatives might be considered as the guardian of the liberties of the people, and therefore ought to have a just proportion to their numbers; but that the Senate represented the sovereignty of the States, and that as each State, whether great or small, was equally an independent and sovereign State, it ought in this branch of the Legislature to have equal weight and authority. Without this, they said, there would be no security for their equal rights, and they would by such a distribution of power, be merged and lost in the larger States.

"This reasoning, however plain and powerful, had but little influence on the minds of the delegates from the larger States; and as they formed a large majority of the Convention, the question, after passing through the forms of debate, was decided that each State should be represented in the Senate in proportion to its population.

"When the Convention had adjourned over to the next day, the delegates of the four smallest States, viz. Rhode Island, Connecticut, New Jersey and Deleware, convened to consult what course was to be pursued in the important crisis at which we had arrived. After serious investigation, it was solemnly determined to ask for a reconsideration the next morning; and if it was not granted—or if, when granted, that offensive feature of the constitution could not be expunged, and the smaller States put upon an equal footing with the largest, we would secede from the Convention; and returning to our constituents, inform them that no compact could be formed with the large States, but one which would sacrifice our sovereignty and independence.

"I was deputed to be the organ through which this communication should be made. I know not why, unless it be that young men are generally chosen to perform rash actions. Accordingly, when the Convention had assembled, and as soon as the minutes of the last sitting were read, I rose and stated the view we had taken of the organization of the Senate, our desire to obtain a reconsideration and suitable modification of that article, and in failure thereof, our determination to secede from the Convention, and return to our constituents.

"This disclosure, it may readily be supposed, produced an immediate and great excitement in every part of the house. Several members were immediately on the floor to express their surprise or indignation. They represented that the question had received a full and fair investigation, and had been definitively settled by a very large majority. That it was altogether unparliamentary and unreasonable for one of the minority to propose a reconsideration at the moment their act had become a matter of record, and without pretending that any new light could be thrown on the subject. That if such a precedent should be established, it would in future be impossible to say when any one point was distinctly settled, as a small minority might at any moment, again and again, move and obtain a reconsideration. They therefore hoped the

Convention would express its decided disapprobation by passing silently to the business before them.

"There was much warm and some acrimonious feeling exhibited by a number of the speakers; a rupture appeared almost inevitable, and the bosom of Washington seemed to labor with the most anxious solicitude for its issue. Happily for the United States, the Convention contained some individuals possessed of talents and virtues of the highest order, whose hearts were deeply interested in the establishment of a new and efficient form of government, and whose penetrating minds had already deplored the evils which would spring up in our newly established republic, should the present attempt to consolidate it prove abortive. Among these personages the most prominent was Dr. Franklin. He was esteemed the Mentor of our body. To a mind naturally strong and capacious, enriched by much reading and the experience of many years, he added a manner of communicating his thoughts peculiarly his own, in which simplicity, beauty, and strength were equally conspicuous. As soon as the angry orators who had preceded him had left him an opening, the Doctor rose, evidently impressed with the weight of the subject before them, and the difficulty of managing it successfully. 'We have arrived, Mr. President,' said he, 'at a very momentous and interesting crisis in our deliberations. Hitherto our views have been as harmonious, and our progress as great, as could reasonably have been expected. But now an unlooked for and formidable obstacle is thrown in our way, which threatens to arrest our course, and, if not skilfully removed, to render all our fond hopes of a Constitution abortive. The ground which has been taken by the delegates of the four smallest States was as unexpected by me, and as repugnant to my feelings, as it can be to any other member of this Convention. After what I thought a full and impartial investigation of the subject, I recorded my vote on the affirmative side of the question, and I have not yet heard any thing which induces me to change my opinion. But I will not conclude it is impossible for me to be wrong. I will not say that those gentlemen who differ from me are under a delusion—much less will I charge them with an intention of needlessly embarrassing our deliberations. It is possible some change in our late proceedings ought to take place upon principles of political justice; or that, all things considered, the majority may see cause to recede from some of their just pretensions, as a matter of prudence and expedience. For my own part, there is nothing I so much dread as a failure to devise and establish some efficient and equal form of government for our infant republic. The present effort has been made under the happiest auspices, and has promised the most favorable results: but should this effort prove vain, it will be long ere another can be made with any prospect of success. Our strength and our prosperity will depend on our unity; and the secession of even four of the smallest States, interspersed as they are, would, in my mind paralyze and render useless any plan which the majority could devise. I should therefore be grieved, Mr. President, to see matters brought to the test which has been, perhaps too rashly, threatened on the one hand, and which some of my honored colleagues have treated too lightly on the other. I am convinced that it is a subject which should be approached with caution, treated with tenderness, and decided on with candor and liberality. It is, however, to be feared that the members of this Convention are not in a temper, at this moment, to approach the subject on which we differ, in a proper spirit. I would therefore propose, Mr. President, that, without proceeding further in this business at this time, the Convention should adjourn for three days; in order to let the present ferment pass off, and to afford time for a more full and dispassionate investigation of the subject; and I would earnestly recommend to the members of this Convention that they spend the time of this recess, not in associating with their own party, and devising new arguments to fortify themselves in their own opinions, but that they mix with members of opposite sentiments, lend a patient ear to their reasoning, and candidly allow them all the weight to which they may be entitled; and when we assemble again, I hope it will be with a determination to form a Constitution—if not such an one as we can individually, and in all respects, approve, yet the best which, under existing circumstances, can be obtained.' Here the countenance of Washington brightened, and a cheering ray seemed to break in upon the gloom which had recently covered our political horizon. The Doctor continued:—'Before I sit down, Mr. President, I will suggest another matter; and I am really surprised that it has not been proposed by some other member at an earlier period of our deliberations. I will suggest, Mr. President, the propriety of nominating and appointing, before we separate, a chaplain to this Convention, whose duty it shall be uniformly to assemble with us, and introduce the business of each day by an address to the Creator of the Universe, and the Governor of all nations, beseeching Him to preside in our councils, enlighten our minds with a portion of heavenly wisdom, influence our hearts with a love of truth and justice, and crown our labors with complete and abundant success!'

"The Doctor sat down; and never did I behold a countenance at once so dignified and delighted as was that of Washington, at the close of his address. Nor were the members of this Convention, generally, less affected. The words of the venerable Franklin fell upon our ears with a weight and authority, even greater than we may suppose an oracle to have had in a Roman Senate. A silent admiration superseded, for a moment, the expression of that assent and approbation which was strongly marked on almost every countenance; I say almost—for one man was found in the Convention, Mr. ——, of ———, who rose and said, with regard to the first motion of the honorable gentleman, for an adjournment, he would yield his consent; but he protested against the second motion, for the appointment of a Chaplain. He then commenced a high strained eulogium on the assemblage of wisdom, talent, and experience, which the Convention embraced—declared the high sense he entertained of the honor which his constituents had conferred upon him, in making him a member of that respectable body; said he was confidently of opinion that they were competent to transact the business which had been entrusted to their care; that they were equal to every exigence which might occur; and concluded by saying that, therefore, he had not seen the necessity of calling in foreign aid.

"Washington fixed his eyes upon the speaker with a mixture of *surprise* and *indignation*, while he uttered this impertinent and impious speech, and then looked around to ascertain in what manner it affected others. They did not leave him a moment to *doubt*—no one deigned to *reply*, or take the smallest notice of the speaker, but the motion for appointing a Chaplain was instantly seconded and carried; whether under the *silent disapprobation* of Mr. ——, or his *solitary negative*, I do not recollect. The motion for an adjournment was then put, and carried unanimously; and the Convention adjourned accordingly.

"The three days recess were spent in the manner advised by Doctor Franklin; the opposite parties mixed with each other, and a free and frank interchange of sentiments took place. On the fourth day we assembled again; and if great additional *light* had not been thrown on the subject, every *unfriendly feeling* had been expelled, and a spirit of conciliation had been cultivated which promised at least a *calm* and *dispassionate reconsideration* of the subject.

"As soon as the Chaplain had closed his prayer, and the minutes of the last sitting were read, all eyes were turned to the Doctor. He rose, and in a few words stated, that during the recess he had listened attentively to all the arguments, *pro and con*, which had been urged on both sides of the House; that he had himself said much, and thought more on the subject; he saw difficulties and objections which might be urged by individual States against every scheme which had been proposed; and he was now more than ever convinced that the Constitution which they were about to form, in order to be *just* and *equal*, must be founded on the basis of compromise and mutual concession. With such views and feelings, he would now move a reconsideration of the vote last taken on the organization of the Senate. The motion was seconded—the vote carried—the former vote rescinded—and by a successive motion and resolution, the Senate was organized on the present plan."

Substantially the same account is given in Southwick's letters on the duty of opening Legislative Assemblies with prayer, as is now done in the National Legislature, and I believe also generally in the Legislatures of the different States. The custom is a testimony to Christianity, which I hope will always be retained. But I am sorry to say that the incident referred to in the history of the Convention cannot be quoted as a precedent. The Observer is deservedly noted for its caution in stating facts. But in this instance, its correspondent is under a mistake in one point. The narrative must have undergone somewhat of a change after it came from General Dayton. The good spirit of the communication shows that if the author has been led into error, he would be thankful to have it corrected. Truth is always the best weapon in vindication of religion; and

I will state the facts as authentic records show them to have actually occurred.

"Veritas non verba magister" was Madison's motto, and we shall have occasion to refer to him as authority. He was a leading member of that memorable Convention, and kept a very minute record of all its deliberations and proceedings, which is now published in the "Madison Papers." He describes the crisis in the Convention on the subject of representation in the Senate, to have become very alarming, and shows that the impending danger was averted by a general spirit of concession and compromise on both sides of the question. On these points he fully agrees with the correspondent of the Observer. They also agree as to the measures proposed by Dr. Franklin for an adjournment, and also for the introduction of religious service by a chaplain. But although the Convention agreed unanimously to the motion for an adjournment, that time might be given for excitement to subside and conflicting views to be reconciled; the motion for inviting a chaplain to open the Convention with prayer *was not carried.* In Franklin's works, we have his speech on the subject, to which a note is appended by himself, stating that his proposition failed; and in the "Madison Papers" we find the history of the whole matter to have been as follows:

The proceedings referred to were on the 28th June; and on that day the determination of the question before the Convention "was put off till to-morrow, at the request of the Deputies from New-York," when Dr. Franklin arose, and said:

"Mr. President,—The small progress we have made after four or five weeks close attendance and continual reasonings with each other—our different sentiments on almost every question, several of the last producing as many noes as ayes—is, methinks, a melancholy proof of the imperfection of the human understanding. We, indeed, seem to feel our own want of political wisdom, since we have been running about in search of it. We have gone back to ancient history for models of government, and examined the different forms of those republics which, having been formed with the seeds of their own dissolution, now no longer exist. And we have viewed modern states all round Europe, but find none of their constitutions suitable to our circumstances.

"In this situation of this Assembly, groping as it were in the dark to find political truth, and scarce able to distinguish it when presented to us, how has it happened, sir, that we have not hitherto once thought of humbly applying to the Father of Lights to illuminate our understanding? In the beginning of the contest with Great Britain, when we were sensible of danger, we had daily prayer in this room for the Divine protection. Our prayers, sir, were heard, and they were graciously answered. All of us who were engaged in the struggle must have observed frequent instances of a superintending Providence in our favor. To that kind Providence we owe this happy opportunity of consulting in peace on the means of establishing our future national felicity. And have we now forgotten that powerful friend? Or do we imagine that we no longer need his assistance? I have lived, sir, a long time, and the longer I live the more convincing proofs I see of this truth—*that God governs in the affairs of men.* And if a sparrow cannot fall to the ground without His notice, is it probable that an empire can rise without his aid? We have been assured, sir, in the Sacred Writings, that 'except the Lord build the house, they labor in vain that build it.' I firmly believe this; and I also believe that without His concurring aid, we shall succeed in this political building no better than the builders of Babel. We shall be divided by our little partial local interests; our projects will be confounded; and we ourselves shall become a reproach and by-word down to future ages. And what is worse, mankind may hereafter, from this unfortunate instance, despair of establishing governments by human wisdom, and leave it to chance, war, and conquest.

"I therefore beg leave to move—that, henceforth, prayers imploring the assistance of Heaven, and its blessings on our deliberations, be held in this Assembly every morning before we proceed to business, and that one or more of the clergy of this city be requested to officiate in that service."

Mr. Sherman seconded the motion.

Mr. Hamilton, and several others, expressed their apprehensions that, however proper such a resolution might have been at the beginning of the Convention, it might at this late day, in the first place, bring on it some disagreeable animadversions; and in the second, lead the public to believe that the embarrassments and dissensions within the Convention had suggested this measure. It was answered by Dr. Franklin, Mr. Sherman, and others, that the past omission of a duty could not justify a further omission; that the rejection of such a proposition would expose the Convention to more unpleasant animadversions than the adoption of it; and that the alarm out of doors that might be excited for the state of things within, would at least be as likely to do good as ill.

Mr. Williamson observed, that the true cause of the omission could not be mistaken. The Committee had no funds.

Mr. Randolph proposed, in order to give a favorable aspect to the measure, that a sermon be preached at the request of the Convention, on the Fourth of July, the anniversary of Independence; and thenceforward, prayers, &c. to be read in the Convention every morning. After several unsuccessful attempts for silently postponing this matter by adjourning, the adjournment was at length carried without any vote on the motion."

From this minute account, the accuracy of which no one will question, it will be seen that, although the motion was not carried, it was not negatived. The Convention disposed of it by adjournment. It will also be seen that those who opposed the motion, did not argue against the principle of having the Convention opened by prayer. They argued from the inexpediency, as they deemed it, of introducing religious services at that juncture in the proceedings of their body. I regret that they should have taken that view of the case. The reply made to their objection by Dr. Franklin and others, ought to have satisfied them. But still there was nothing in their opposition that can be justly termed avowed irreligion or wanton mockery of the Most High. Had the wise proposition been made when the Convention first assembled, in all probability it would have been passed unanimously.

How far the deliberations of the Convention might have been aided, had Dr. Franklin's advice been taken, it is not for man to say. But admirable as our Federal Constitution is, and unwise as it would be to disturb or derange its great principles, time has shown that it was not so perfect when first formed as to preclude amendment. The speeches delivered on its adoption, prove that some leading members of the Convention were not entirely satisfied with it themselves. When Dr. Franklin arose to move that it should be signed by the members, he said: "I confess that there are several parts of the Constitution which I do not at present approve, but I am not sure I shall never approve them; the opinions I have had of its errors, I sacrifice to the public good. Within these walls they were born, and here they shall die." His hopes, however, seem to have brightened when he saw the general unanimity that prevailed in the Convention before their final adjournment. Mr. Madison relates that "while the last members were signing, &c., Franklin, looking towards the President's chair, at the back of which a rising sun happened to be painted, observed to a few members near him, that painters had found it difficult to distinguish in their art, a rising from a setting sun. I have," said he, "often and often, in the course of the session, and the vicissitudes of my hopes and fears as to its issue, looked at that behind the President, without being able to tell whether it was rising or setting; but now, at length, I have the happiness to know, it is a rising, and not a setting sun." And the sun has been rising ever since. The clouds which at times have obscured its face, have neither arrested nor delayed its upward course. The nation cannot be too thankful to Him "by whom princes decree justice," that the great bond of her Union, the Constitution as it now stands, has led her to a growth in power and wealth which has fully proved its wisdom and excellence; and if prayer was not offered *by* the Convention who framed it, prayer was offered *for* them, during all their deliberations, by thousands of Christians throughout the whole nation.

Although this note has already reached an unusual length, I may perhaps be excused if I extend it still farther.

There is a deep sentiment of reverence for the fathers of the Republic pervading the mind of the nation, which is to be counted among the best signs of our times; and as the value of the Union cannot be too strongly urged, especially at the present juncture of public affairs, every friend of his country will feel an interest in seeing how these venerable, wise and upright men felt and spoke on the subject when it came before them in their deliberations. They were statesmen of the right stamp, ornaments, not only of their country, but of their age. They possessed enlarged minds, capable of appreciating the influence of their deeds on the destinies of their own nation and of the world.

A great object of the Federal Convention, as it is usually termed, was to perpetuate and strengthen an Union of the States; so to combine their resources as to promote national prosperity and greatness. The former Confederacy had been found entirely inadequate to meet the wants of the country; and as the Convention was called to meet a crisis which involved the best interests of the nation, the several

States showed a studious care to select as their delegates men of tried worth and ability. We find upon the roll not only Washington, who was unanimously called to preside over its deliberations, but also such men as Rutledge and the two Pinckneys, (Charles and Charles Cotesworth,) from South Carolina, Randolph and Madison from Virginia, Martin and Carroll from Maryland, Franklin with Robert and Gouverneur Morris from Pennsylvania, Paterson and Livingston from New Jersey, Hamilton and Lansing from New-York, Sherman and Ellsworth from Connecticut, King and Gorham from Massachusetts, with others who had figured conspicuously for their statesmanship and patriotism. Resolutions, as the basis of a Constitution, were laid before the house by Mr. Randolph; and "the object of the proper plan," to be considered, was declared by Mr. Madison "to be twofold;—first, to preserve the Union; secondly, to provide a Government that will remedy the evils felt by the States both in their united and individual capacities." In the progress of the Convention, as already stated, the difficulty, of reconciling the conflicting claims of the smaller and larger States was found to be almost insurmountable, and on several occasions a rupture seemed inevitable. Every thing was seen to depend upon a spirit of forbearance and concession; and a dissolution of the Union was deprecated, as an evil to be avoided by every sacrifice.

"Let the union of the States be dissolved," said Mr. Madison, "and one of two consequences must happen. Either the States must remain individually independent and sovereign; or two or more confederacies must be formed among them." * * * * "Either event," he afterwards declared, "would be truly deplorable; and those who might be accessory to either could never be forgiven by their country or by themselves."

In view of such a contingency, Mr. Gorham conceived—

"That a disruption of the Union would be an event unhappy for all; but surely the large States would be the least unable to take care of themselves, and to make connections with one another. The weak, therefore, were most interested in establishing some general system for maintaining order. If, among individuals composed partly of weak, and partly of strong, the former most need the protection of law and government, the case is exactly the same with weak and powerful states. * * * * On the whole, he considered a union of the States as necessary to their happiness, and a firm General Government as necessary to their union. He should consider it his duty, if his colleagues viewed the matter in the same light as he did, to stay here as long as any other State would remain with them, in order to agree on some plan that could, with propriety, be recommended to the people."

Among "the consequences of a dissolution of the Union" Mr. Hamilton predicted,

"Alliances will immediately be formed with different rival and hostile nations of Europe, who will foment disturbances among ourselves, and make us parties to all their own quarrels. Foreign nations having American dominion are, and must be, jealous of us. Their representatives betray the utmost anxiety for our fate, and for the result of this meeting, which must have an essential influence on it. It had been said, that respectability in the eyes of foreign nations was not the object at which we aimed; that the proper object of republican government was domestic tranquillity and happiness. This was an ideal distinction. No government could give us tranquillity and happiness at home, which did not possess sufficient stability and strength to make us respectable abroad. This was the critical moment for forming such a government. We should run every risk in trusting to future amendments. As yet we retain the habits of union. We are weak, and sensible of our weakness. Henceforward the motives will become feebler, and the difficulties greater. It is a miracle that we are now here, exercising our tranquil and free deliberations on the subject. It would be madness to trust to future miracles. A thousand causes must obstruct a re-production of them."

Mr. Gouverneur Morris

"Wished it to be understood that he came to the Convention

as a representative of America; he flattered himself he came here, in some degree, as a representative of the whole human race; for the whole human race will be affected by the proceedings of this Convention. He wished gentlemen to extend their views beyond the present moment of time; beyond the narrow limits of the place from which they derive their political origin. If he were to believe some things which he had heard, he should suppose that we were assembled to truck and bargain for our particular States. He cannot descend to think, that any gentlemen are really actuated by these views. We must look forward to the effects of what we do. These alone ought to guide us."

The Constitution having been finally adopted in the Federal Convention, was yet to be sent down for ratification to the several States, with the provision as expressed in Article VII, that "the ratification of the Conventions of nine States should be sufficient for the establishment of the Constitution between the States, so ratifying the same." State Conventions were accordingly brought together to act upon the subject. The debates which took place in these several bodies, together with other documents of public interest, have been collected with much care by Elliott, and published in four volumes. His reports of what occurred in some of the Conventions are brief and imperfect, as he had to depend chiefly on cotemporary publications. But in other cases his account is very full and satisfactory. His report of the debates in the Convention of Virginia fills his entire third volume. When the question was submitted to that body, the decision was admitted to be of paramount importance, as the Constitution had already been ratified by eight different States; and the ratification by Virginia would be conclusive on its final adoption for the government of the nation. The Convention itself was much divided in sentiment. The eloquent Patrick Henry led a powerful opposition; and it was not a little remarkable that the leader on the other side was Governor Edmund Randolph, who was one of the three that had declined to sign the Constitution when finally adopted in the Federal Convention. Subsequent reflection seems to have satisfied his mind that the welfare of the country demanded the ratification of the instrument as it then stood; and that amendments which he and others thought desirable, should be left to be afterwards introduced according to the mode prescribed in the Constitution itself.

"As with me," he said, "the only question has ever been, between previous and subsequent amendments; so will I express my apprehensions, that the postponement of this Convention, to so late a day, has extinguished the probability of the former without inevitable ruin to the Union, and the Union is the anchor of our political salvation; and I will assent to the lopping of this limb (meaning his arm) before I assent to the dissolution of the Union."

In the progress of the debate we find him on one occasion declaring,

"Were I convinced that the accession of eight states did not render our accession also necessary to preserve the Union, I would not accede to it, till it should be previously amended: but, sir, I am convinced that the Union will be lost by our rejection. Massachusetts has adopted it; she has recommended subsequent amendments; her influence must be very considerable to obtain them. I trust my countrymen have sufficient wisdom and virtue to entitle them to equal respect. It is urged, that being *wiser* we ought to prescribe amendments to the other states. I have considered this subject deliberately, wearied myself in endeavoring to find a possibility of preserving the Union without our unconditional ratification; but, sir, in vain. I find no other means * * * I have every reason for determining within myself, that our rejection must dissolve the Union; and that our dissolution would destroy our political happiness."

In the course of his arguments he observed,

"We are now inquiring particularly whether Virginia, as contra-distinguished from the other states, can exist without the Union. A hard question, perhaps, after what has been said. I will venture, however, to say, she cannot. I shall not rest contented with asserting—I shall endeavor to prove."

In the conclusion of this powerful speech, he said,

"I shall conclude with a few observations which come from my heart. I have labored for the continuance of the Union—the rock of our salvation. I believe that, as sure as there is a God in Heaven, our safety, our political happiness and existence depend on the union of the states; and that without this union, the people of this, and the other states, will undergo the unspeakable calamities, which discord, faction, turbulence, war, and bloodshed, have produced in other countries. The American spirit ought to be mixed with American pride to see the Union magnificently triumph. * * * * * Let it not be recorded of Americans that, after having performed the most gallant exploits—after having overcome the most astonishing difficulties—and after having gained the admiration of the world by their uncomparable valor and policy, they lost their acquired reputation, their national consequence and happiness, by their own indiscretion. Let no future historian inform posterity that they wanted wisdom and virtue to concur in any regular efficient government. Should any writer, doomed to so disagreeable a task, feel the indignation of an honest historian, he would reprehend and recriminate our folly, with equal severity and justice. Catch the present moment; seize it with avidity and eagerness, for it may be lost, never to be regained. If the Union be now lost, I fear it will remain so for ever."

While the subject was under discussion, and one gentleman after another was called out, Mr. Corbin declared,

"By Union alone can we exist; by no other means can we be happy. Union must be the object of every gentleman here. I never yet have heard any gentleman so wild and frantic in his opposition as to avow an attachment to partial Confederacies.

By previous adoption, the Union will be preserved: by insisting on alterations, previous to our adoption, the Union may be lost, and our political happiness destroyed by internal dissensions."

When the deliberations were drawing towards a conclusion, some gentleman in the opposition having hinted a purpose to retire from the Convention, and go home, Governor Randolph appealed to them,

"I beg to make a few remarks on the subject of secession. If there be, in this house, members who have in contemplation to secede from the majority, let me conjure them by all the ties of honor and duty to consider what they are about to do. * * * * Such an idea of refusing to submit to the decision of the majority is destructive of every republican principle. It will kindle a civil war, and reduce everything to anarchy and confusion."

Feeling the responsibility which he had assumed in urging the adoption of the Constitution, although ably seconded by Madison, Marshall, Nicholas, Pendleton, Corbin and others; at the close of the Debate, he pled,

"Mr. Chairman, one parting word I humbly supplicate: The suffrage which I shall give in favor of the Constitution, will be ascribed, by malice, to motives unknown to my breast. * * * Lest, however, some future annalist should, in the spirit of party vengeance, deign to mention my name, let him recite these truths —*that I went to the Federal Convention* with the strongest affection for the Union; that I acted there in full conformity with this affection; *that I refused to subscribe, because I had, as I still have, objections to the Constitution*, and wished a free inquiry into its merits; and that the accession of eight states reduced our *deliberations* to the single question of *Union, or no Union*."

Although the Reports of the proceedings and debates in the other Conventions are, as we have said, comparatively brief, yet they are sufficient to show that the attachment to the Union, so triumphant in Virgina, was also the predominant feeling in the other States, and especially the States in the South. In the Convention of North Carolina, Mr. Iredell was a leading man. He urged the ratification of the Constitution, arguing,

"By adopting it we shall be in the Union with our sister states, which is the only foundation of our prosperity and safety. We shall avoid the danger of a separation, a danger of which the latent effects are unknown. So far am I convinced of the necessity of the Union, that I would give up many things against my own opinion to obtain it. If we sacrificed it by a rejection of the Constitution, or a refusal to adopt, (which amounts, I think, nearly to the same thing,) the very circumstance of disunion may occasion animosity between us and the inhabitants of the other states, which may be the means of severing us for ever."

In the Legislature of South Carolina, the proposition to call a State Convention was warmly opposed by Mr. Lowndes, and some others; but it was supported by the Rutledges, the Pinckneys, and such men as Pringle, Mathews, Barnwell, Read and Ramsay. During the discussion Mr. Charles Cotesworth Pinckney said,

"Without union with the other states, South Carolina must soon fall. Is there any one among us so much a Quixote as to suppose that this State could long maintain her independence, if she stood alone, or was only connected with the Southern States? I scarcely believe there is."

Having afterwards referred to the Declaration of Independence with high encomium, he proceeded,

"In that Declaration the several states are not even enumerated; but after reciting in nervous language and with convincing arguments, our right to independence, and the tyranny which compelled us to assert it, the Declaration is made in the following words:—'We, therefore, the representatives of the United States of America, in general Congress assembled, appealing to the Supreme Judge of the world for the rectitude of our intentions, do, in the name, and by the authority of the good people of these colonies, solemnly publish and declare, that these United Colonies are, and of right ought to be, FREE AND INDEPENDENT STATES.' The separate independence and individual sovereignty of the several states were never thought of by the enlightened band of patriots who framed this declaration; the several states are not even mentioned by name in any part of it, as if it was intended to impress this maxim on America, that our freedom and independence arose from our union, and that without it we could neither be free nor independent. Let us then consider all attempts to weaken this Union, by maintaining that each state is separately and individually independent, as a species of political heresy which can never benefit us, but may bring on the most serious distresses."

The Convention having been called; on the second day after it met, Mr. Charles Pinckney delivered a speech of great power and eloquence, which seems indeed to have precluded any considerable debate during the subsequent deliberations. Alluding to some of the leading features of the Constitution, he said,

"In their individual capacities as citizens, the people are proportionably represented in the House of Representatives; here, they who are to pay to support the expenses of government, have the purse-strings in their hands; here the people hold and feel that they possess an influence sufficiently powerful to prevent every undue attempt of the other branches, to maintain that weight in the political scale which, as the source of all authority, they should ever possess: here, too, the states, whose existence as such we have often heard predicted as precarious, will find in the Senate the guards of their rights as political associations.

"On them. (I mean the state systems,) rests the general fabric: on their foundation is this magnificent structure of freedom erected, each depending upon, supporting, and protecting the other; nor, so intimate is the connexion, can the one be removed without prostrating the other in ruin: like the head and the body, separate them and they die.

"Far be it from me to suppose that such an attempt should ever be made. The good sense and virtue of our country forbid the idea: to the Union we will look up, as to the temple of our freedom—a temple founded in the affections, and supported by virtue of the people; here we will pour out our gratitude to the Author of all good, for suffering us to participate in the rights of a people who govern themselves.

"Is there, at this moment, a nation upon earth that enjoys this right, where the true principles of representation are understood and practised, and where all authority flows from, and returns at stated periods to the people? I answer, there is not. Can a government be said to be free where these rights do not exist? It cannot. On what depends the enjoyment of these rare, these inestimable privileges? On the firmness, on the power of the Union to protect and defend them.

"How grateful, then, should we be, that, at this important period—a period important, not to us alone, but to the general rights of mankind—so much harmony and concession should prevail through the states—that the public opinion should be so much actuated by candor and an attention to their general interests—that disdaining to be governed by the narrow motives of state policy, they have liberally determined to dedicate a part of their advantages to the support of that government, from which they received them. To fraud, to force, or accident, all the governments we know have owed their births. To the philosophic mind, how new and awful an instance do the United States, at present, exhibit in the political world! They exhibit, sir, the first instance of a people, who, being dissatisfied with their government—unattacked by foreign force, and undisturbed by domestic uneasiness—coolly and deliberately resort to the virtue and good sense of their country for a correction of their public errors.

"It must be obvious, that without a superintending government, it is impossible the liberties of this country can long be secured.

"Single and unconnected, how weak and contemptible are the largest of our states! how unable to protect themselves from internal or domestic insult! how incompetent to national purposes would even partial union be! how liable to intestine wars and confusion! how little able to secure the blessings of peace?

"Let us, therefore, be careful in strengthening the Union—let us remember that we are bounded by vigilant and attentive neighbors, who view with jealous eye our rise to empire."

These were the deliberate and enlightened views of the

sages and patriots who laid the foundations of our national greatness. Being dead, they yet speak. Their sepulchres are with us to this day; and in all periods of agitation which put in jeopardy the Institutions they framed for us, we should reverence their memories, and seek counsel from their wisdom. Especially should we turn to Him with a filial regard whom we all delight to honour as "First in war, first in peace, and first in the hearts of his countrymen," and who has left us this memorable warning in his Farewell Address:

"*It is of infinite moment that you should properly estimate the immense value of your national union to your collective and individual happiness; that you should cherish a cordial, habitual, and immovable attachment to it; accustoming yourselves to think and speak of it as the palladium of your political safety and prosperity; watching for its preservation with jealous anxiety; discountenancing whatever may suggest even a suspicion that it can, in any event, be abandoned; and indignantly frowning upon the first dawning of every attempt to alienate any portion of our country from the rest, or to enfeeble the sacred ties which now link together the various parts.*"

END OF NOTES.

www.ingramcontent.com/pod-product-compliance
Lightning Source LLC
LaVergne TN
LVHW010227110826
845151LV00004B/1209